ABOUT MUSH

Mush is the fastest-growing social app for mums in the UK. Launched in April 2016 by Katie Massie-Taylor and Sarah Hesz, two London mums who met in the playground and became each other's lifeline during maternity leave, Mush has now become the most wide-reaching social app for mums in the UK and Australia. They have one mission: to make being a mum more sociable and fun.

Their editor Isabel Mohan has been part of Team Mush from the start and has shaped the content on the app in terms of tone of voice and range of content. Isabel started her career on *Heat* magazine fifteen years ago, leaving after six years to launch the *Daily Mirror*'s 3 am gossip site before going freelance in 2012, writing on entertainment and women's lifestyle for the *Telegraph* and *Grazia*, among others.

THE MUMSITION

YOUR FRIENDLY COMPANION TO THE FIRST YEAR OF MOTHERHOOD

ISABEL MOHAN, KATIE MASSIE-TAYLOR,
SARAH HESZ

piatkus

PIATKUS

First published in Great Britain in 2018 by Piatkus

1 3 5 7 9 10 8 6 4 2

A CIP catalogue record for this book
is available from the British Library.

ISBN 978-0-349-41745-5

Illustrations © Josephine Dellow

Typeset in Stone Serif by M Rules
Printed and bound in Great Britain by
Clays Ltd, St Ives plc

Papers used by Piatkus are from well-managed forests
and other responsible sources.

Piatkus
An imprint of
Little, Brown Book Group
Carmelite House
50 Victoria Embankment
London EC4Y 0DZ

An Hachette UK Company
www.hachette.co.uk

www.improvementzone.co.uk

ACKNOWLEDGEMENTS

This book wouldn't have been possible without the hundreds of brilliant mums who came forward with hilarious, moving, reassuring and, above all, personal stories about their experiences of early motherhood. You know who you are and we are forever grateful. Even for the bits that made us wince and cross our legs.

Also a big thank-you to our families and, of course, our kids, who brighten up our days and ruin our nights. You're the best.

Finally, this is for all the mums on Mush. You show us every day how a network of support, caffeine-fuelled early morning buggy walks and tantrum-tastic teatime play dates can totally transform motherhood for the better. See you by the swings.

CONTENTS

INTRODUCTION

Hello, you. OK, so we could have said 'Hello, Mum', but you'll soon find out that one of the weirdest and most infuriating bits of new motherhood can be the fact that you no longer feel like you have a name. We promise we'd use yours if we knew it!

You're going to meet a lot of new people over the next few months – health visitors asking you questions about bodily fluids, baby sensory teachers waving tie-dye scarves in your face, baristas who ply you with caffeine when you really, really need it and oh, the big one, *your baby!* – but among the most important figures in your life will be all the other mums you cross paths with.

Other mums know exactly what you're going through, from the relentless sleepless nights to the joys of that first gummy smile; other mums are just as bogged down in all things baby as you, and are there to analyse the weird grunty noises your newborn makes at night, but also there (ideally with some wine on hand) to help you feel like you again – albeit a you whose life has changed rather a lot.

Mush started because two tired mums, Sarah and Katie, who were right in the thick of it, met in a rainy playground, realised they had loads in common, spent every day together from then on and decided that friendships like theirs shouldn't all be down to chance encounters. So, despite no tech experience and four under-twos between them, they invented an app. Hundreds of thousands of mums around the world now use Mush to make friends with other mums in the same boat, all going through perhaps the biggest life change ever: The Mumsition.

Early motherhood can make your head explode, especially when it comes to the sheer amount of information you're bombarded with from antenatal courses, parenting forums, instructional books and random old ladies in the supermarket. It can be overwhelming, so we've rallied together our mum mates to bring you what you really need: easy-to-digest advice and anecdotes, many of which will hopefully get you laughing when you're feeling overwhelmed – or at least make you nod in recognition and realise you're not the only one going through all this.

We know that rekindling your relationship with your partner, getting to grips with your post-baby body and simply deciding what to do when you've got cabin fever can be just as tough as dealing with a colicky newborn, so everything in the book has *you* in mind, as much as your baby. Your baby's great, of course, but you're way more interesting than they are right now.

We hope you're enjoying your Mumsition!

Team Mush x

1

Thirty-six weeks pregnant

When your life is about to get turned upside down *for ever*

And relaaaaaax. Ha. As if. OK, so you're nearly at the end of your pregnancy and you've probably wound down at work, which means you're very much entitled to a lovely sit-down. But – and it's a big but – we know how hard this can be in practice.

Should you be bouncing around on a birth ball, washing tiny clothes over and over again, getting as much sleep as possible while you can (whoever invented that particular cliché has clearly never manoeuvred a giant, uncomfortable, bladder-squishing bump into bed), getting as little sleep as possible to get you used to it, batch-cooking, getting your bits waxed, painting the radiators because you noticed a minuscule chip and you've gone nesting-crazy, or all of the above? And how are you meant to fit in all that when the only thing you can think about is how you're going to get the baby out?

Yep, it's a bloody exciting time, but, chances are, your brain has never been so busy. While the first trimester was all about nausea, knackeredness and deception, and the second trimester was all about taking bump selfies and wondering what happened to the boundless energy you'd been promised, the tail-end of the third trimester is a heady mix of feeling physically drained but emotionally amped up. The day when you'll meet your baby is tantalisingly close, you wake up at weird times and you find yourself going from feeling over-prepared to under-prepared in the blink of an eye.

The best advice we can give you right now? Basically, ignore all the advice! Do what you can to close yourself off from all the noise, because there's more than enough of it in your own head, and try to do something nice for yourself every day. With everything we're about to say, we promise we aim to 'inspire' you, rather than instruct you ...

Five things to do right now because it could be your last chance for eighteen years

Look, we don't want to freak you out but your life as you know it is about to change *for ever*. Here are a few suggestions for the stuff you should get out of your system right about now ...

1. Go to the cinema with your partner

Baby cinema – where you go and watch proper grown-up films with a gurgling baby on your lap – is great, it really is, and we whole-heartedly recommend it as one of the activities you should do when your baby is tiny (more on that later). But baby cinema is not relaxing or romantic.

When your currently unborn baby is older and you're ready to reclaim your social life, you'll probably find that going to the cinema is quite far down on the list of things you might feasibly bother to get a babysitter for. Instead, weddings and big birthday parties and date nights involving food and booze will be prioritised. Because you can always watch films at home.

But going to the cinema somehow always feels like a special treat – a treat that is ideal for a heavily pregnant woman who can't drink much booze but can definitely inhale a vat of popcorn or sweets (heartburn permitting, although there's always ice cream – it's practically medicinal). Turn it into even more of a treat by going to one of those posh cinemas with sofas that you can doze off on.

2. Get your hair done

There are mobile hairdressers, and hairdressers who don't mind babies, but neither feel quite like the pampering experience of going to a fancy-pants salon and staring at your own bloated reflection for two hours and/or reading trashy magazines. As close to your due date as possible, book yourself in for a 'do'.

If you're overdue, even better: booking appointments is a sure-fire way of nudging your body into labour, just to mess with your day. Soon every day will be messed with, so it's good practice.

3. Go shopping

We appreciate that if you're currently wielding an enormous bump, you probably don't much feel like hauling it around a shopping centre. But you know who else hates shopping centres? Babies. And toddlers. And just kids generally, actually, until they become teenagers, when they will develop a love of shopping centres, but won't be seen dead in them with their embarrassing old mum.

So go shopping asap, for you. Now is not the time to be trying on clothes, but why not go to a department store and get your make-up done, or buy nice things for your house because you are going to be spending a lot of time in it soon, and that clock or teapot or lamp you've always been indifferent to will start to really irritate you, and you'll wish you'd idly browsed for a nicer one when you had the chance.

Sure, you can buy things for the baby too, if it makes you happy, but the main purpose of this exercise is to treat yourself.

4. Lie down and read a book

Ooh, this is meta, since you are literally reading a book right now. But controversially we're going to tell you to put this book down every now and again and read some fiction that has nothing to do with babies. If, like many of us, you've made a list of wonderful books to get lost in on maternity leave, we hate to break it to you but: *never gonna happen, babes*. When you become a mum, it's impossible to think about anything other than your baby, so the only things you'll read will be books about having a baby (hi!) and Calpol packaging. 'But I'll read when the baby sleeps!' you cry. Nah. You'll look at photos of the baby while the baby sleeps, because you'll miss them so much.

5. Have a night out with your best friends

This one's important. You might not feel much like going out on the razz, but having a grown-up night with your friends, even if it's just going for dinner at someone's house, is crucial. Sure, you'll still see your friends when you have a baby – especially in the early weeks when there'll be a queue of them at your door desperate for cuddles – but it becomes really, really hard to organise anything, especially if some of them have kids too.

Plus, even when get togethers do happen, you'll be so distracted by the baby clinging onto you, or indeed so distracted by the fact that you've actually left the baby with someone else for seventy-six minutes, that you won't be able to have a decent conversation.

So arrange something now – eat something delicious, drink something expensive (just the one, obvs), wear something ... tent-like, and talk like it's going out of fashion. You might be tired, but you won't regret it.

WHAT OUR MUM MATES SAY

I was 38 weeks pregnant on our first wedding anniversary and didn't massively feel like going out (due to feeling massive!), but I'm so glad I did because now I feel nostalgic for being able to go out without having to factor in a babysitter! We just went to a local Italian restaurant (which we kind of ended up naming our baby after ...) and it was blissful – well, until the heartburn kicked in ...

Izzy, mum of two

We moved house four days before my C-section – the ultimate nesting activity but obviously a little bit stressful and not something I'd recommend to everyone! The best bit was trying to retrieve one of our cats from the top of a nine-foot wardrobe in our old flat. I didn't have a cat box so I had to wrap her in a cardigan and jump in a taxi. One plus side to moving house while 39 weeks pregnant is that nobody expects you to do any heavy lifting though.

Nicky, mum of two

Don't plan to do too much. I now know that the best thing about leaving work a month before my due date was having the luxury of being a bit bored!

Raji, mum of one

Clothes: how to turn your baby into a fashion icon ... or what you actually need to buy before they're born

One of the most fun and exciting things about the late stages of pregnancy is getting all the insanely cute and tiny clothes ready for your little one. It's tempting to go absolutely nuts and buy enough stuff to clothe octuplets, but your baby really only needs a capsule wardrobe to start with ... their future career as an Instagram influencer won't start until they've got past the awkward flaky newborn skin stage, so no point blowing the wardrobe budget now.

Do buy/borrow/blag:

At least ten vests Get long-sleeved and short-sleeved vests – in newborn size and nought to three months (in case you birth a whopper). The word 'vest' in baby clothes terms is confusing – they're not actually what one would usually call a vest, but basically tops with a crotch. They're sometimes called bodysuits too, and you'll find that, whatever the season and time of day, they form the axis of every outfit.

On a scorching hot day, a short-sleeved vest is all your newborn needs. When it's chilly, a long-sleeved one is the ideal first layer. Teamed with leggings, they're a comfy, practical outfit, so make sure you get some jazzy ones as well as plain white. Your baby will then look stylish enough to go straight from the office to the bar. Wait, we're getting carried away with this fashion thing – we mean straight from the playmat to the Moses basket.

At least five pairs of leggings/joggers Basically dress your baby as if they're going to a yoga class, with an emphasis on comfy, easily removable layers. Leggings with feet are particularly brilliant (especially if you plan to carry your baby in a sling) because baby socks are basically the most irritating thing in the world.

A couple of hats You need one soft, stretchy, lightweight hat (mainly for covering up how weird their head looks when they've just been born and you're desperate to send people photos) and, depending on season, either one cosy winter hat or sunhat. That's it. After all, how many hats do you have of your own? One or two? Definitely not twenty in every colour of the rainbow and a few more besides. Always remember, your baby is a regular human being, not a member of East 17.

A couple of lightweight zip-up jackets and/or cardies Once again, it's all about comfort and layering. You want hoodless hoodies (because hoods themselves get in the way and you'll worry about them getting tangled up) and cardigans to put over vests on a warm day or under a coat on a cold one. Top tip: if you haven't got a family member who knits, we recommend hanging around your local old people's home while heavily pregnant. Smile a lot, buy biscuits *et voilà*: a wardrobe full of stylish knits. OK, probably not that stylish. But useful.

Don't buy/borrow/blag:

Too many sleepsuits Some people keep their newborns in sleepsuits 24/7, but you still don't need that many, because *everyone* will buy them for you. Plus, you might prefer to put them in 'proper' clothes (vests and leggings ...) after a few weeks. So, just get enough sleepsuits for night-time (say, a couple of multi-packs from the supermarket – they're usually surprisingly good quality and come in cute prints) and you'll probably find your selection multiplies fast.

Too many socks and mittens They'll need a few pairs of socks, especially if they're a winter baby, but generally baby socks fall off constantly, as do scratch mitts (just trim their flipping nails already!). A twenty-minute walk with a baby in a sling can take an hour when their stupid socks fall off so many times that you end up going hunting for them, like a really tedious version of *Hansel and Gretel*. Also, you're going to have loads of laundry as it is – do you really want to throw dozens of tiny things that need pairing up into the mix? Leggings with feet are the way to go.

Baby shoes People will buy you baby shoes, especially tiny replicas of grown-up trainers, but you will rapidly realise that the only thing more annoying than baby socks is baby shoes. They don't stay on their feet and – we hate to break it to you – no matter how super-advanced your precious newborn most certainly is, they definitely can't walk yet.

A massive puffy snowsuit Of all the cute, tiny things, snowsuits are basically the cutest tiny thing of all. They're also largely unnecessary in this country when your baby is still immobile. They're far too hot and stifling if, for instance, you're going in and out of shops. If you're going for a walk outside with the pram it's more practical to layer up with vests, a cardi, normal coat and blankets, because you can easily take stuff on and off as needed. Snowsuits are also a big no-no for the car seat, since you won't be able to tighten the straps properly and they take ages to get on and off. They're pricy too, so avoid for now and go snowsuit crazy when they're a toddler (and look so cute that you will want to eat them).

Kit: what you really need to throw money at for your impending arrival

Oh, pregnancy, such a pure, innocent, natural time, as you float around dreamily on a cloud of contentment and Gaviscon. Well, it's *all lies*. You're not a precious vessel – you're an advertiser's dream. People will constantly try to sell you 'essential' baby items, preying on the fact that you're an enthusiastic rookie who just wants a baby who sleeps/smiles/ looks cute. Put the PayPal password away and read this first.

You might not need: a changing bag
Instead: get a rucksack

You have probably already wasted several evenings (um, definitely not whole *days* at work) hunting online for a stylish changing bag to store all those nappies and wipes and teeny weeny, ickle wickle vests. Newsflash: there is no such thing.

Changing bags generally look a bit twee, and they're pretty cumbersome. Rucksacks look cooler, hold more stuff and you probably have one already. Plus, if you ever end up carrying your baby in a sling, a changing bag isn't just annoying, it's plain unusable. Another option is to buy/blag/borrow one of those handy little 'changing pouches' that slip inside any bag. So, don't blow a fortune on a monster changing bag just yet – consider borrowing or getting one preloved from a local mums group – and use your cash to buy more teeny weeny, ickle wickle vests instead. Way cuter – and you'll definitely use them.

You might not need: a Moses basket for naps
Instead: get a stretchy wrap sling

People who think a baby will be 'spoilt' if it's held too much are very silly indeed. Were you also spoiling it by reluctantly agreeing to carry the clingy little parasite in your womb for nine months?

There's a reason your newborn wakes up every time you plonk it in a basket because you want to 'get things done'; it's cold and empty in there! An option that's more likely to restore calm is to bung him or her into a cosy, stretchy wrap and go about your business while they nap like a dream. We'd recommend hitting up your local sling library to find one that works for you before committing to buying one (especially because some babies don't get on with them). But bear in mind the only business you need to go about when you've just had a baby is all eight seasons of your trashy teen drama of choice.

You might not need: a travel cot
Instead: get real. You ain't going nowhere anytime soon

Sure, you'll need a travel cot in the future, but they're definitely surplus to requirements for newborns who don't do much in the way of sleeping in beds, let alone in a big shiny prison that smells of camping.

The ones with newborn attachments are really expensive, and barely get used, because tiny babies whose ages are still defined in weeks prefer sleeping somewhere familiar (in fact, who doesn't prefer sleeping somewhere familiar?). You're better off getting one of those portable sleep pod thingies or a pram with a carrycot attachment that's cleared for night-time sleeping, since, if you do go and stay with relatives (or, God forbid, go on actual holiday), you'll likely be taking that with you anyway.

You might not need: overpriced breastfeeding clothes
Instead: get nice pyjamas

If you're planning to breastfeed, you'll gradually suss out how to make your wardrobe work around that hungry newborn, whether it's by wearing stretchy vests under t-shirts, wrap dresses over crop-tops or, please don't do this, taking scissors to your best silk blouse.

In the early days, you won't be going out much anyway. So, instead of buying up the internet's entire selection of peephole tunics, treat yourself to some nice button-down PJs and relish being a slob.

You might not need: a dedicated baby bath
Instead: get in the water yourself

Baby baths, even the foldable ones, take up valuable space in the smallest room in the house and are a pain to fill and empty. There's no reason why your baby can't use the main bath from day one, and sharing a bath with your newborn is the loveliest bonding experience. They'll feel safe and secure in your arms and – bonus! – when you're struggling to fit showers into your day, you'll stink a bit less too.

NB: This is best tackled when your partner's around to help you and baby get out when you're done though – freshly washed newborns are slippery little creatures.

You might not need: a baby monitor
Instead: get loads of extra media storage

It's going to be at least a couple of months before your baby sleeps anywhere other than a few inches from you, so you don't need to shell out for a baby monitor just yet – wait for a hand-me-down or really good deal.

In the meantime, if you're simply gagging to spend money on gadgets, why not buy a shared external hard drive or similar so that, when you inevitably photograph and film every second of your baby's day, you have somewhere to back it all up. Our mum friend who left her phone on the roof of her car and lost every picture she'd taken for the first six months of her daughter's life wishes she'd thought of this ...

WHAT OUR MUM MATES SAY

I wouldn't bother with reusable nappies for newborns – I was full of good intentions but used them twice because I just couldn't be arsed. Also, books on how to get your baby to sleep and be happy – I was too tired to read them!

Alice, mum of three

During a bad sleep phase I bought some sort of automatic baby rocker that cost nearly £100. Total waste of space! We ended up leaving it outside a charity shop under the cloak of darkness ...

Freda, mum of two

Those scrapbooks to keep as mementos just made me feel guilty that I'm not a better parent. When my kids ask when they got their first tooth/word/whatever, I'll probably just lie. We got about five as gifts and they're very sweet but seriously, don't give a new mum homework!

Sara, mum of two

My advice for mums to be would be only to buy the absolute essentials at first – just what they need to wear, sleep in and be carted around in – and figure out what else you actually need as you go along. Unless you live in Outer Mongolia, local selling pages and online shopping will sort you out pretty quickly.

Rosie, mum of one

I signed up to an eco-nappy laundry service that provided the nappies and then took them away to wash them. I never remembered to use them, so I put fake soiled disposable nappies (just wees, not poos – although I did consider it) in the collecting bin and left it outside the front door, then hid behind the sofa clutching my baby whenever the nappy man came calling. This went on for months and felt sane at the time.

Ellie, mum of three

The five stages of choosing a baby name

Picking baby names is fun – in theory. Most of us have a secret list of names in our head (or, we admit it, saved in our actual phones) for our imaginary baby, way before we've even found the person we'll make one with. But that doesn't mean said person will agree. And there are a whole lot of other things to think about too.

1. The initial brainstorm

This is the fun bit, and might well be one of the first things you did when you found out you were pregnant: leafing through baby name books, browsing mum forums, delving into the family history for any surprise inspo, reading through the credits on TV shows, and drawing up a longlist of names – perhaps before you know if you're having a boy or a girl. But beware, this is the honeymoon period of name-choosing.

2. The existential crisis

You then start analysing your list and questioning who you even are. Do you want a name from the top-twenty list from last year so that your little one will always fit in, or do you want to show how unconventional you are by picking something unusual? You work in the legal department of a large bank – can you really pull off cute nature names like River and Willow? Or you like traditional names like James and Charlotte, but now you're worried this makes you really boring? The last thing you want to do is seem trendy or faddy, so you scrub any names on the list that seem to tick that box, leaving you with … no clue, no clue at all. Remember, all that really matters is that you (and your partner – but more on that shortly) like the name. What it conveys to other people you know is largely irrelevant (unless you're thinking of calling them Princess Consuela Banana-Hammock; then might we gently suggest a small rethink?).

3. The tense negotiations

Guess what? It turns out your partner might want some input into this whole name thing too. The cheek of it! OK, so modern etiquette dictates that you, the owner of the vagina that will eject the baby (or indeed the torso that will be sliced open to eject the baby), will likely get the final say, but, in the name of equality, your partner should also be allowed to veto any names they don't like. They might even make some suggestions of their own, and we would urge you to pretend to politely consider at least half of them, instead of spitting out your stir-fry and openly scoffing at their plain ludicrous suggestions.

4. The fear

So, you finally think you've found the name. But the period between choosing the name and the baby actually being born can be a tense one. Every time you scroll your social media feed and see that a celebrity – especially if it's one you find a bit naff – announces a new arrival, you will shakily click on the link, terrified that they will have stolen your name. And it's much, much worse if you have actual friends or relatives who are expecting a baby too, especially if theirs is due a few weeks before yours. You won't be able to relax about this until your baby is born and you've announced it to everyone. Which leads us on to ...

5. The reveal

We strongly recommend not sharing your name of choice with anyone until the baby has been born. You'll feel irritated if a friend or family member fails to disguise their disgust at the 'ridiculous' name you've chosen, but they are far less likely to do this if it's already attached to a tiny, beautiful human whom they now love. When you announce the name, you can also be smug in the knowledge that all the people you know who are slightly less pregnant than you were are now reading it with the same trepidation you recently felt. But you've bagsied it now – unless you looked at your baby when they were born and realised the name you'd settled on didn't suit them at all. In which case it's back to square one, but a lot more frantically this time.

WHAT OUR MUM MATES SAY

We had settled on a lovely name and middle name combo for our little girl ... but then I made the mistake of googling it and discovered it was the name of a brothel in Australia. I tried to put this out of my head, given that the only people who'd realise this would have to be familiar with the brothel in question, in which case they were probably unlikely to mention it. And hey, if she goes travelling when she's older, maybe she can have her picture taken outside it!

Lucy, mum of two

We have two girls, and really struggled to choose a name for our second, especially because I spent most of the pregnancy convinced we were having a boy. It sounds silly but it felt sort of mean to give her one of the names we'd discarded for our first, so we had to come up with a whole new list. In the end, she was a couple of days old before we finally agreed on one, and even then I wasn't sure at first. Now, of course, she couldn't be anyone else!

Nicky, mum of two

I thought we'd chosen a pretty unusual name for our little boy, but when he was a few weeks old and I started taking him along to baby groups, I realised how wrong I was. There are loads of them! It's since appeared as one of the fastest climbers on the baby name lists, which makes me feel like I was unwittingly part of a fad. Even my next-door neighbour has used the same name. If I'm honest, I'm a bit gutted about it all, although at least he won't get picked on for having a weird name ...

Caz, mum of one

Spoiler alert: a few things you should know before the baby arrives

We don't want to ruin the surprise, but there's some stuff you should probably brace yourself for.

The weird things your body's doing now are just the tip of the iceberg

Of course, when you're pregnant, you expect to grow a great big, beautiful bump, but the other twists and turns of your body can come as more of a shock. Body hair does strange things (thicker in places, thinner in others), the hair on your head does even stranger things (mainly shedding massively and alarmingly in the early months of motherhood. Don't panic, it grows back!), you might get freckles for the first time, your feet could go up a size – and stay there – and your bladder control will leave a lot to be desired for quite some time (*pelvic floor reminder!*), along with your mystical milk-making boobs and your magical elastic tummy. Remember, you are a thing of wonder and don't let anyone make you feel otherwise.

Over the next couple of years you will buy seven buggies and five car seats (approx)

During pregnancy you'll obsess over picking the right, eye-wateringly expensive pram – sorry, 'travel system' – which will last your precious firstborn for years, can glide smoothly along urban roads and woody trails and exotic beaches and has multiple recline functions, as well as being compatible with your similarly eye-wateringly expensive, state-of-the-art car seat.

But ... once your baby is getting on for a year or thereabouts, you'll find this lovingly chosen contraption a bit cumbersome and trade it in for a bog-standard, more acceptably priced buggy. You might get an even more lightweight stroller for nursery runs/holidays, or maybe a double buggy further down the line, and even a running buggy if you're a Sporty Spice. Then you'll wonder why you wasted all those hours (days, weeks) of research on something that was mostly just good for the newborn days. But all that research is a good distraction and feels like a way of getting control over the craziest thing that's ever happened to you, so go with it, bank balance permitting.

Late-pregnancy heartburn can be just as bad as early-pregnancy morning sickness

Just like not everyone gets morning sickness, not everyone gets heartburn. Or, at least, not severe heartburn that puts you right off your takeaway. But for anyone in the thick of it (are you digesting this book with a side order of Gaviscon?), it can be just as debilitating – especially since one of the perks of pregnancy is supposedly being able to eat lots of food, then, all of a sudden, it's the last thing your stupid, burning gullet can handle.

The one upside is that, by the point that heartburn likely kicks in, everyone knows you're pregnant anyway, so you can luxuriate in moaning about it, rather than having to pretend to be hungover like you did in the early days of feeling like death in the office loos. Plus, it goes away as soon as you've given birth (to be replaced by an altogether different burning sensation – but more about that later).

There's no point in worrying about sleep

Your baby might be a good sleeper, they might be a terrible sleeper; it's mainly luck of the draw, but the best (but, possibly, hardest) thing you can do is try not to fret about it. Realise that sleep goes up and down throughout the early years, based on all manner of factors, and not your ability as a parent.

Your life is about to change, big time, but you'll be so in love with your new arrival that you won't mind how knackered you are, as long as you're kind to yourself (by which we mean: biscuits). You'll get used to your new routine (or lack of) and time with a newborn goes so fast that, before you know it, they'll be fourteen and refusing to get out of bed before midday. This is the time to put Steve Wright's *Sunday Love Songs* on top volume and throw in a bit of lawn mowing for good measure.

You really, really need mum friends

You might think 'I've got loads of mates!' but unless your bezzies all live under ten minutes from you and are all due to give birth at exactly the same time, you'll need some new mum friends too – for early-morning park circuits, poo banter, emergency wines and emergency whines.

It's hard to understand the value of finding people in exactly the same situation until you're right in the thick of it, but whenever you need a friend, remember: Mush is full of like-minded mums with kids the same age – go get 'em!

Kickstarting labour: things to try and myths busted

If you're overdue and fed up with this whole pregnancy business – and who can you blame you, it is *long* – you might be mulling over ways you can get that baby to make an entrance. Trying a few old tricks can be a good way to pass the time, but your baby won't come along until it jolly well feels like it.

Sex

Oh man, do we have to? Well, no. But if you're gagging to get that baby out, you should know that semen is rich in prostaglandins (the very thing used in inductions), so if you can find it in your heart to make sweet, functional love, it could be worth a go. That's assuming your humongous bump allows access.

Nipple stimulation

Even less appealing than sex when you're so flipping pregnant? Probably. But nipple stimulation – and realistically we're talking hours and hours of it – can cause a surge in oxytocin, which starts contractions. You may be some time, so make sure there's something good on the telly and perhaps take it in turns with your partner to do the twiddling, so you don't get RSI.

Curry

Well, getting a takeaway or even going out for dinner is certainly a good distraction, but the reality is, food that's so spicy it could stimulate your uterus is unlikely to be something you fancy right now – especially in the required quantities to actually make a difference.

Pineapple

The theory is that pineapples (as well as a few other tropical fruits) are rich in bromelain, which can have a ripening effect on your cervix. Again, you'd need a hell of a lot of it to really make a difference – a little juice box or a Hawaiian pizza probably won't cut it.

Complementary therapies

Massage, reflexology and acupuncture can all be recommended to bring on labour, but there's little scientific evidence that they actually work. If you happen to go into labour straight afterwards, it's likely, as with most of these methods, to just be a coincidence. But you deserve a bit of pampering (we're thinking massage more than needles here), so why not?

Eating dates

This is one you need to plan ahead for, because there is some evidence – from an actual scientific study, no less – that eating six dates a day in the final month of pregnancy can encourage your cervix to dilate. This is more likely to shorten labour than actually kickstart it, though, so proceed with caution.

Raspberry leaf

Similarly, raspberry leaf – either in capsule or tea form – can tone your womb muscles, encouraging them to work more effectively. However, it should never be taken before your baby is full term (thirty-seven weeks) and should be used in moderation, since too much could cause your contractions to be unbearably intense.

Moving around a lot

Walking more and boinging around on a gym/birthing ball are all worth a go, the theory being that being upright and active puts the right kind of pressure on your cervix and potentially stimulates contractions. You might feel like festering on the sofa, but try to get a bit of jiggle time in each day.

WHAT OUR MUM MATES SAY

We booked a fancy curry at a local, very reputable Indian restaurant and kept dropping cheeky hints to the waiters that this might be the meal that brought the baby on, in the hope that we'd get a freebie. Neither happened that night ...

Lynda, mum of one

I read somewhere that rubbing a point on your ankles could be used to induce labour. With our second baby, I got my husband to rub it really hard and had given birth within twelve hours, so I was convinced it was magic. Tried it with our third ... no sign for ten more days.

Alice, mum of three

I drank raspberry leaf tea by the gallon, even though it's not actually that nice. When I was finally in labour, I went into the kitchen, called it a bastard and threw it in the bin because oh my God, the unimaginable pain!

Sara, mum of one

Both my babies came once I'd spent some time cuddling other people's newborns. I reckon babies have psychic abilities to chat to each other in the womb. Joke! Maybe it's something to do with hormones.

Reem, mum of two

I tried every trick in the book ... but guess what? None of them worked. I even bought five different types of cheese to make this ridiculous aubergine parmigiana recipe from an American restaurant which claimed it was responsible for bringing on hundreds of labours. I was so desperate to avoid induction that if someone had told me to roll in fox poo for an hour, I probably would have done ...

Ru, mum of one

2

The big day (or days)

When you've actually got to get the thing out

O. M. G. We hate to come over all hysterical pubescent girl but *you're about to have a baby!* Squeeeeeeeeeeeeeal!

OK, glad we got that out of our systems. Now, the serious stuff: there's a giant baby currently in you, and you need to get it out. And that, despite being 'the most natural thing in the world', is no mean feat. Whether you're a 'give me all the delicious drugs' type or you're planning to breathe your baby out, the main issue is that even the most blissful birth never goes a hundred per cent to plan. And thinking about that can be scary.

We're about as medically qualified as Doctor Seuss, so we're not going to get into the nitty-gritty of it all; instead, we want to give you a bit of an overview of all the things that might happen and share the experiences of a variety of real mums, to reassure you that everything you're worrying about is totally normal, and you probably won't remember any of it when you've got your baby in your arms.

The A to Z of giving birth

A is for anaesthetic, in the form of an epidural

In the weeks before giving birth – after grilling mums you know, going to antenatal classes and consulting Dr Google on an alarmingly regular basis – you'll probably have developed some preferences about whether or not you want pain relief, and, if so, what kind. Lots of mums write in their birth plans that they *do not* want an epidural, because they don't like the idea of not feeling anything. Some stick to this; others scream *'Give me an epidural!'* when they don't really like the feelings in question after all. You won't always get one, though: sometimes, by the stage you're in this much pain, it's too late for pain relief. The good news is, this means the baby's coming really soon.

B is for Braxton Hicks

The opposite of your baby coming really soon, Braxton Hicks are pesky fake contractions which can kick in sporadically about halfway through your pregnancy. They can escalate later on, and have sent many a first-time mum trotting off to the hospital, convinced they're the real deal.

C is for contractions

The real deal. To start with, they're like period pains. They end up being a liiiiiittle bit more intense than this. But we don't want to ruin the surprise.

D is for doula

Not just for hippies, doulas are an extra person to have around during and after the birth. They'll have your back when it comes to your preferences and generally bring the chilled vibes. And possibly some scented candles.

E is for episiotomy

If your midwife thinks your baby is going to struggle to make it out (what with, you know, being about a million times bigger than your vagina) or is already in distress, one of these – a surgical cut to your bits, followed by stitches – might be strongly recommended. The thought might make you cringe, but you're pretty likely to tear anyway; this is just a more controlled way of doing it.

F is for forceps

Not forgetting their good friend Ventouse. Forceps are the giant tongs, Ventouse is the vacuum-cap thing. They serve similar purposes: getting your baby out safely when you or they are struggling. Nobody but nobody wants them, but they're a safe option and remember: everyone just wants to deliver your baby safely.

G is for gas and air

A delicious concoction that can send you to a higher plane during labour – if it works for you. If it doesn't, you might just puke and ask for the hard stuff.

H is for home birth

It's not as simple as just blowing up the birth pool and getting on with it; if you fancy a home birth, you'll have put hours of planning into it and will be understandably disappointed if you end up going to hospital after all. An unplanned home birth is a different kettle of fish – but it's rare in first-time mums, since labour tends to start slowly. But not always.

I for irritated

Plenty of things might irritate you while you're in the throes of labour. Your partner for tapping their foot erratically (anyone would think they were nervous), the midwife for not magicking your baby out of your fanny, inanimate objects for touching you, the lights in the delivery suite for being so damned bright ... This is your time to be a massive diva. You will be forgiven.

J is for juice

You'll want to stay hydrated and energised during the birth, and juice boxes with straws are a winner, as are isotonic drinks. It's called labour for a reason and you need all the energy you can get.

K is for ketamine

What you might accidentally ask for when you really mean pethidine (see **P**). Pretty embarrassing, let's pretend it didn't happen.

L is for looooong

Unfortunately, this ordeal can go on for days. It's definitely going to go on for hours. But you get a nice baby at the end of it, hurrah.

M is for midwife

Your new best friend and worst enemy. But really she's your best friend. If your labour is one of the looooong ones, you might meet several, since it turns out they have lives of their own and don't work forty-eight-hour shifts. Afterwards you'll feel bad for not remembering all of their names.

N is for naked

You might have a birth outfit all planned out, but when it comes down to it, all that material flapping around could well annoy the hell out of you, and you'll just want to be in your birthday suit. Your baby will be turning up naked too, so you might as well set the dress code.

O is for orgasm

Some women claim to experience orgasms during birth. Most don't.

P is for pain and pethidine

Which sounds a bit like a Jane Austen novel but most definitely isn't. Hippy types don't like the word 'pain' to be used about giving birth, preferring to liken it to 'sensations'. But we can sensationally reveal that it is quite painful, unfortunately. Pethidine is one way to numb that pain – it's a morphine-esque painkiller that will be injected into your thigh, should you demand it. It can make you feel rather spaced out, so not all women like the idea.

Q is for queen

We don't mean to come over all Beyoncé, but this is *you*! You're birthing a baby! You're amazing!

R is for ring of fire

A jolly little song by Johnny Cash; a not so jolly sensation that you might experience as your baby crowns. But try to think of it as exciting, yeah? They're nearly here! *Owwwwww, holy hellfire!*

S is for skin-to-skin

What you'll be encouraged to do as soon as you've given birth, as long as all is well. And it's absolutely lovely ... even when your shiny new human enjoys the closeness so much that they immediately wee on your thigh.

T is for TENS machine

A jazzy little machine that can help with pain relief in the early stages. We'd recommend borrowing or renting one, since you're unlikely to need it for long (well, until the next time). Also a good distraction for your partner when they're fannying around, desperate to make themselves useful.

U is for umbilical cord

These days some people like to delay cutting the cord; if it's wrapped round your baby's neck, this won't be an option. It's attached to the placenta, which is bigger and grosser than you ever imagined.

V is for vomit and other bodily fluids

Many women puke during labour; others also wee and poo and generally lose all control of their bits and their inhibitions. It's normal and the midwives have seen and smelled it all before. Just make sure you've brought plenty of clean clothes for afterwards.

W is for water birth

Loads of mums want one, not everyone gets one – either because there are no pools available or because there are medical reasons why it's not advised. If you're planning to have one, remember to ask if a sieve is provided or if you need to bring your own (see **V**, above).

X is for eXciting

All of this might sound pretty intense, but it's also the most exciting thing that's ever happened to you. You're about to be a mum! You can think happy thoughts about this during the small moments of respite and relaxation between contractions.

Y is for yodels

Some of the noises you make while in labour might sound like you're yodelling. Others might sound like a wild animal. Others might sound like the worst swear words you've ever heard, which is a good reason to not have your mum as your birth partner.

Z is for zero

This is precisely how many shits you'll give about everything that's just happened when you hold your beautiful baby in your arms for the first time. Same time next year, then?

WHAT OUR MUM MATES SAY

The two births that I had at home in water were as good as they could be. Deep breathing in through the nose and then exhaling really slowly and loudly through teeth to keep oxygen flowing, stay calm and help ride the contractions. Sips of chilled juice through a straw at regular intervals helped my dry mouth and kept my energy levels up. I had annoyingly straightforward births so sorry if all that just sounds like I attended a tough Pilates class!

Ellie, mum of three

No, your waters haven't broken. You're just horribly sweaty.

Katherine, mum of one

If there are things that are important to you, like being active rather than flat on your back, rehearse saying those things and get your partner on board in case labour turns you into a spineless jelly. I didn't do this, and found myself meekly complying with what they told me to do – and then things started to go pear-shaped.

Rosie, mum of one

Why the hospital bag is just a distraction – but here's what you should put in it anyway

Secret fact that only mums know: lots of the things that you're encouraged to think about and plan and obsess over while pregnant are all a big ruse. Picking the right pram (real talk: all prams are basically the same and all basically annoying), spending hours constructing a birth plan and packing the hospital bag are all just distractions to help you feel a tiny bit in control of something that's fundamentally uncontrollable.

That said, planning and packing and unpacking and packing your hospital bag again is a good use of time when you're waiting to pop. Some of the stuff that goes in might even get used. Oh, and 'hospital bag' is misleading – you'll probably end up taking a wheely suitcase, two hold-alls and three Bags for Life spilling out with crap. Here's what you actually need.

For you

- A laptop or tablet with pre-downloaded entertainment (do not blow your phone data on Netflix!) in case you're in for the long haul. The trashier the better – now is not the time for hard-hitting Danish dramas.
- Headphones. So that the whole maternity ward doesn't need to know that you watch *Geordie Shore*. And so that you don't have to involuntarily eavesdrop on the woman in the next bay's annoying mother-in-law.
- Phone charger. On the off-chance that you want to send people the odd photo of *the cutest baby in the world*.

- Hair ties. Otherwise you may find yourself screaming that you want to shave your head immediately.
- Flip-flops, sliders or slippers. Base your decision on the season, although bear in mind that hospitals are always absolutely boiling.
- Stretchy bra tops. The really cheap kind that come in multi-packs. They're comfy and super-stretchy, so work well as sleep/nursing bras, as well as drying super-quickly after a water birth if you have one.
- Wrapped snacks. Think cereal bars, dried fruit, sweeties, stuff that doesn't go off or make too much mess. Shove some chocolate in there too, just because – although it might melt due to aforementioned tropical climate of most hospitals.
- A comfy nightie or big t-shirt, plus a dressing gown. Depending on how long you're in, you might want a few nightwear options – especially because you'll inevitably get gross bodily fluids on them.
- A pillow. Because the hospital ones can be stingy. Also useful when you're trying to get to grips with feeding.
- Loads of pants. And then some more pants as well. Big old comfy ones.
- Maternity pads. Useful for when your waters break, as well as all the mess afterwards. Take more than you think you need!
- Travel-size toiletries. (Remember face wipes – you might not have a face full of make-up to wipe off, but they'll help you feel cool and fresh.)

For the baby

- Nappies, obvs.
- Nappy paraphernalia. Midwives will tell you your baby's bum must be cleaned with cotton wool and boiled water to start with. Very few people actually keep this up. Proceed with caution as babies do have sensitive skin, but these days there are plenty of very gentle wipes on the market, including the reuseable variety, if you can be bothered.
- Clothes. Consider packing newborn size *and* the next one up, in case you birth a whopper (you have our sympathies).
- A hat. Partly for warmth, partly for aesthetic reasons due to aforementioned tendency for newborn heads to be a bit misshapen and/or crusty to start with.

For your partner

- Whatever they might need for an overnight stay, in case they end up stopping over. A toothbrush is definitely a good call, because babies can smell fear.
- A list of people to contact with the news, along with the words '*Tell them not to put anything on Facebook until we have*' underlined in red.
- A can-do attitude and lots of patience – see the next chapter ...

WHAT OUR MUM MATES SAY

Pack a few more things than you planned for yourself. I ended up being sick on myself during labour and only had my outfit I wore there and my going home outfit – I was in for a week. I also totally didn't realise how many pads I would need – you can never have too many pads!

Stephanie, mum of one

Pack snacks but ... this is the crucial bit – *do not forget to eat the snacks!* Your midwife will forget to remind you to snack because she's pretty busy attending to your bits. You and your partner will forget to snack because being in labour is quite distracting. And if you do not snack, you'll feel sick, gas and air will make you nauseous, the birthing pool will make you vomit and pethidine will make you vomit on a nurse. And your first words on the birth of your child will be 'Can I have a Starburst please?'

Helen, mum of one

Most ladies go into labour at night and I read somewhere it has to do with mammal instincts where dark = safe. When you go into hospital the bright lights can really mess with this. This might sound silly but take a pair of sunglasses! I also took headphones to block out all the hospital noise.

Rupi, mum of two

Six important jobs for your partner (disclaimer: you might still swear at them)

It's tough being a birth partner ... said no mum ever. OK, so pushing half a stone (give or take a few pounds) of baby out of your body is incomparable to any other life event and, sadly, no matter how many game men attempt to simulate labour pains in the name of YouTube lols, unless you've actually given birth, you will never understand what it really feels like.

But still ... it's a difficult time for them too. You might feel out of control – but they're properly helpless, witnessing the person they love most in the world going through a whole range of new emotions and sensations. They're scared – possibly more scared than you, due to the aforementioned lack of control thing – and nervous about 'getting it wrong' and upsetting you. But, the truth is, they can't really get it wrong (unless they bugger off to watch *Match of the Day* while you're crowning) since, when it comes to giving birth, we're all really just making it up as we go along.

Sweeping generalisation: everyone enjoys feeling useful and helpful, so here are a few ways you can get them involved while you get on with the small matter of bringing a whole fricking human being into the world using your body. Yeah, yeah, you're kind of busy here, but there's no harm in helping them help you.

1. TENS technician

TENS machines can be a godsend – sure, they can help with pain relief particularly during the early stages but, more importantly, they are a great distraction. Getting your partner to take control of the strength of the vibrations will make them feel genuinely useful, even further down the line when you suspect that that little machine is no longer doing much. It's the ultimate piece of practical help, and feels a bit like playing a video game. A really painful video game.

2. Entertainment manager

Many of us fixate on the music that will be playing when we give birth, spending hours crafting the perfect playlist and even forking out for portable speakers because we don't trust the hospital to provide them, only to completely forget about the whole thing when we're actually giving birth. Putting your partner in charge of the entertainment situation will make them feel useful and supportive – plus, they'll enjoy geeking out over it anyway.

3. Butler

You've packed some snacks in your hospital bag, of course, but, if you have a long labour, you may find yourself having random culinary whims at the hospital. Suggest that your partner does a reccy beforehand so that he knows exactly where he can get that suddenly crucial cup of tea/dirty burger/Slush Puppie, should the mood take you. Bonus points if he also offers biscuits to midwives.

4. Chief liaison officer

Best case scenario, nobody else knows you're in labour yet. But if you're having a scheduled induction or C-section, or you went into labour at work (it happens!), or you just had to tell your mum because she's your mum, chances are there will be unsolicited comms flying in from all directions. This can be extremely annoying for you, especially if things are taking longer than you'd hoped (suddenly the seemingly inno- cent words 'Any news yet?' will seem like *the* most annoying in the English language), so hand your phone over and let your partner send any genuinely necessary messages* on your behalf.

---

* This may include asking your neighbour to feed the cat/water the plants/put the bins out, because you may be here for some time.

5. Official spokesperson

Remember that birth plan you drew up? Well, it might be the furthest thing from your mind when you're actually in the thick of it, but make sure your partner is aware of the stuff that's really important to you so they can relay it to the midwives when needed. However, they also need to know that they should button it if you really, really change your mind about pain relief.

6. Therapist, Samaritan, Punchbag

Contrary to televisual depictions of birth, many women are actually quite nice to their partners during labour, what with them, hopefully, loving them and what-not. But there will be stressful moments where your partner bears the brunt of it. The best thing they can do in this situation is listen, definitely *not* try to offer helpful suggestions, and then implement a 'what happens in labour stays in labour' policy for afterwards. This also applies to anything gross they see. And they *will* see gross things. And probably joke that the placenta would go down well with a bit of barbecue sauce.

WHAT OUR MUM MATES SAY

I had a huge hospital bag and even remembered to pack bendy straws. However, I somehow forgot pants for after the birth, so my husband nipped out to the nearest shop to the hospital – and came back with an extra-large pair of men's boxers, because it was all he could find. He also once mistook my actual pants for a Moses basket fitted sheet, but that's a whole other story ...

Lynda, mum of one

I got really frustrated with my husband when my first was born by emergency caesarean. He couldn't find anything in the hospital bag and kept getting the wrong things out, and I couldn't bend down to help due to the stomach situation. Second time round, I packed the whole lot in labelled freezer bags to make it easier for him, e.g. 'newborn vests', 'big pants', 'things to make me smell nice'. It took the stress away and I enjoyed my smug organised parenting ... for the first and last time ever.

Kate, mum of two

Six tips on giving birth the old-fashioned way

Contrary to all the horror stories the internet throws at us, most births do actually start by themselves and go reasonably smoothly. Sure, it hurts. And sure, it can go on a bit. But you get a lovely prize at the end (a baby – and maybe some vaginal stitches). Here are a few pointers.

1. Remember that things can happen in no particular order

Some women have a bloody show – that's when the delightful mucus plug ejects itself – but this can happen days before proper labour begins, so it can be a cruel tease. Some women's waters break before anything else. Some people have an upset tummy for days. Labour can start in a variety of different ways and at first you'll question it. If you're a control freak, it's hard to just go with the flow and let nature take its course, but no amount of googling will make things go a different way – just focus on the fact that the baby's coming, yay! The baby! Is coming!

2. Don't rush to the hospital

First-time mums often get sent away from the hospital – potentially even more than once – because they're not in quite enough labour to justify a hospital bed. This can come as a surprise, but chances are you're just getting started. Make the most of your time at home while contractions are bearable. Watch telly, have a bath or, more likely, pace around wondering if you've forgotten to buy various items that suddenly seem life-changingly essential (chill – twenty-four-hour super-markets and Amazon Prime exist for a reason).

3. Trust your instincts

Midwives are amazing, but amazingly busy. Once you are actually allowed in the hospital, it doesn't mean you're going to get anyone's undivided attention. But, if nobody's examined you for a while because you've been bobbing along nicely without requiring much assistance, and suddenly you can feel things accelerating, you may have to demand some you-time. This is the one time in your life you can get away with being a bit of a diva, so make the most of it – nobody judges in the labour ward! They have seen it all before and far, far worse.

4. Embrace the grossness

You might be sick all over yourself and on several bystanders. You might poo without realising it. There are definitely going to be some bodily fluids floating around, perhaps more than you ever imagined. This is an ongoing theme of motherhood, so this is basically a preview of the next year/eighteen years of your life. Enjoy!

5. Forget everything

From the playlist you prepared for labour to the hair bobbles you just know you brought with you, along with the small matter of the 'birth plan', if only you could remember which of your seven bags they're in. There are things that will totally pass you by while you're in the moment. And it doesn't matter at all. Once again, your inner control freak needs to just roll with it.

6. Cry 'I can't do it!'

No matter how smoothly your labour goes, at some point you will think, and probably say, the above. It's a rite of passage, which is why you might notice the midwife smirking.

WHAT OUR MUM MATES SAY

Perineal massage made a huge difference for me. I was keen to avoid a fanny catastrophe so I made the poor husband do it every other night from 34 weeks right up to going overdue to 42 weeks, because I couldn't manage it myself – my massive bump was in the way! I had a long labour but afterwards the midwife inspected the goods and I just had a small graze. I know it doesn't work for everyone but it's worth a try because for me it was definitely worth it. And it's something to do as you count down the weeks!

Emma, mum of one

Don't download a contraction tracking app. Mine said 'call an ambulance' – which we didn't – but we did rush to the hospital and when we got there I was only 2cm dilated. I just had unusually long and frequent contractions from the start – yay!

Anna, mum of one

First-time labours can be fast, despite the fact that so many books and classes tell you you'll be having niggles and twinges for days. I was 9cm only two and a half hours after my first (massive!) contraction which was scary because I hadn't expected things to move so fast. I thought it must mean there was something wrong, but now I know I'm just a fast labourer and there's no time for messing about in the bath at home!

Eimear, mum of two

Six tips on being induced

Nobody sets out to be induced – but don't let that pessary make you pessimistic.

1. Do not google

Here are the most important words you'll read if you've just been booked for an induction: put the smartphone down. Why? Because if you search for information about inductions, you'll end up on message boards where despairing women are begging for 'positive induction stories please!!!!', but nobody's providing them. Instead, all you'll see is the words 'spiral of intervention' because while that pessary might look innocent enough, if it didn't work, then there'd be the dreaded drip, and then maybe the even more dreaded emergency C-section.

But remember, people don't tend to go on forums to say,

'my induction was entirely unremarkable'. Get the medical info from your midwife, ignore all the anecdotes and go with the flow.

2. But do adjust your expectations

OK, so that blissful home birth, where your angelic newborn glides into the world while you sip Prosecco in a candlelit pool with Enya personally serenading you from a beanbag, isn't going to happen.

Whether you're being induced ahead of your due date for medical reasons, or you're a poor, tired overdue whale, your induced labour will be a little bit medical from the outset. You'll probably be in hospital for a few days and you'll be monitored more than you might like. But, all being well, you can still walk around, and you can still have a relatively natural birth.

3. Line up some entertainment, you may be some time

Before you go in, fill your device of choice with trashy films and boxsets to watch while you wait for the hormones to take effect. Hospitals generally don't have (free) Wi-Fi and now is not the time to blow a fortune on data add-ons from your phone.

It's not as if you can concentrate on reading a book when you're confined to an antenatal ward, waiting for your life to change for ever, surrounded by multiple impatient inpatients. You need headphones and you need distracting trash.

4. Set your birth partner free

You don't need your partner hanging around the hospital while you wait to go into labour. Unless they have particularly under-standing employers, it will eat into their parental leave and give you less time together when the baby's actually been born.

They'll also be just as bored as you, and they'll moan about it, but nobody will be fiddling with their genitals at regular intervals, and this will annoy you. Ideal scenario: while you wait for the damn baby to rev into action, they work from home, rather than miles away, and pop in regularly with snacks, encouragement and extra knickers.

5. Keep your eyes on the prize

The good news about induction is that, whatever happens, your baby will be along very soon indeed. Sooner than if nature took its course.

Pregnancy is a flipping marathon, but this bit, even if it takes three days and doesn't go according to plan, is a mere jolly little sprint, promise. Ish.

6. Sorry, but . . . do a poo. Just do one

Look, we're all grown-ups, we can talk about poo. Once that baby's born, it will be all you talk about, so we might as well start now.

Fact: when the pessary's up there, you might feel a bit paranoid about going to the loo, in case it somehow falls out. So, try to go beforehand, OK?

WHAT OUR MUM MATES SAY

I was induced with both children because I went so over-due. It was disappointing but at the time, I was so over being overdue that I was just pleased to be getting on with it. And, do you know what? It was OK – the first time. Thanks to having an epidural, I was able to have a six-hour sleep before I started pushing! The second time was a bit more nuts, but all fine in the end. But I don't know it any other way and who knows if it was better or worse than if I'd gone into labour naturally?

Katie, mum of two

I was induced at 39 weeks because I had high blood pressure. Being in and out of hospital getting my blood pressure checked all the time was annoying and stress-ful, so I was quite relieved about the possibility of not being pregnant anymore! And my experience was totally fine – the worst part was just that there was a lot of sitting around. It took a couple of days, two pessaries, the gel and, finally (and most helpfully, I think), a particularly prob-ing 'examination' from a consultant with *massive* hands before I went into labour, presumably because my baby was perfectly happy where he was, but once my waters broke – all over the hospital corridors and lift, FYI, since I'd been encouraged to roam around, it was really fast. I managed with just gas and air and it felt pretty natural. So try not to pay attention to all the horror stories about loads of interventions – it honestly doesn't happen to everyone.

Izzy, mum of two

Six tips on having a C-section

Whether it's what you wanted all along, it's been scheduled due to complications, or you end up having an emergency one, there are a few things that will make the whole under-the-knife thing go a bit more smoothly ...

1. If it's elective: take advantage of the ability to plan

Unfortunately this doesn't apply to last-minute or emergency caesareans, but if you've got it scheduled in good time, you can really make the most of your pre-baby maternity leave, get everything ready at home, swan around getting your hair/toenails/online banking done and generally look forward to your appointment with your baby. Of course, there *is* the possibility that you'll go into labour naturally before the big day (especially because these days they tend to be around thirty-nine weeks, to make sure the baby is as well-cooked as possible. It's a risky game!) but we won't think about that, yeah?

2. Expect it to feel a bit surreal

All being well, due to the amazing power of anaesthetic (modern medicine, you are incredible), it will just feel vaguely like you're having a lie down while some nice efficient medical staff play pass the parcel behind a screen. You will then be presented with a baby. How did that happen? It just did.

3. Don't feel guilty

Lots of mums – especially those who were hoping to pop out the baby, trad style – feel guilty about having C-sections. Whether elective or emergency, it's happening for a damned good reason – the baby's health, your physical health and/or your mental health. Never forget this.

4. Take all the drugs

You've just had major surgery. A paracetamol probably isn't going to cut it. If you're in a lot of pain, don't suffer in silence – this is what liquid morphine is for. Always ask if you think you need more of the good stuff. Don't try to be a hero.

5. Know that recovery gets easier fast

The first few days post C-section can be agony – mind you, so can the first few days post-vaginal birth – but it's incredible how quickly you'll go from feeling battered to just feeling slightly sore. That said, don't overdo it – now is your time to make the most of resting, as you're not going to get much of it over the next year or ten.

6. Get all the help you can

All new mums need support, but if you've had a C-section, physical help from your partner, friends and family is essential. Say yes to every offer (even if allowing your mum to do your food shopping simply means you just get a bit of alone time with your partner and baby. And even if she does buy the wrong kind of teabags, *again*). It can be upsetting if you can't even lift your baby without assistance but, honestly, this part will be over in a flash.

WHAT OUR MUM MATES SAY

The whole vibe of my C-section was very cheerful – even the handsome surgeon who sounded like a gameshow host when he asked, 'Are you ready to meet your baby?' Afterwards, a nurse said, 'Well done, she's a big girl,' which felt strange since I didn't feel like I'd done anything. Overall, I felt really well looked after, like there were a lot of very skilled and caring people doing their best for me.

Nicky, mum of two

Don't try to do too much when recovering even if you feel OK. Take time and all the help offered. And stick a maternity pad in the front of your enormous granny pants to give extra support for your scar!

Rowena, mum of three

How not to freak out when things don't go according to plan

The whole process of conceiving and growing and birthing and raising a child is fraught with surprises. There are good surprises, like when you finally see the two lines on the pregnancy test after three, six, twelve months or more of trying, and funny surprises, like your baby being born with a full head of hair, and disgusting surprises, like the first time they do a poonami on a packed train.

And then there are the bad surprises. If you've struggled to conceive, been through baby loss or generally had a rocky road to get to where you are now, you'll understandably approach the birth with more trepidation than most. Once you get to the looks-like-she-could-pop-at-any-moment stage of pregnancy, everyone around you will be reassuring you that you're out of the woods and saying – rightly – that it's highly unlikely that anything will go wrong now, but still you'll worry. It's all totally normal and the best thing you can do is talk to other mums about it. You'll find out that they're experiencing all the same emotions and fears. Hooray for solidarity in anxiety, eh? But if you think that your worries are getting the better of you, it's always best to broach it with your midwife or doctor for reassurance and practical support, because approaching labour gripped by fear won't do you any favours.

But no matter how 'sorted' you feel about the whole giving birth situation, and how many hundreds of pounds you've thrown at hypnobirthing teachers and mindfulness podcasts, unfortunately things don't always go according to plan.

Veering off your birth plan is to be expected even in the most straightforward of births, and anything that needs to happen is for a very important reason: everyone present just wants your baby to be delivered as smoothly as possible.

There are a million twists and turns your labour can take – here are a few of the most common (and perhaps the ones you're most anxious about). But just remember – most births go pretty smoothly. You hear horror stories because people like telling them – far fewer people go on parenting forums or regale their acquaintances with long-winded dramatic anecdotes about their totally average birth. But every day plenty of women are having them, we promise.

You wanted a home or birth-centre birth but have ended up in hospital

If your home birth doesn't happen, it's gutting, but it's also likely to be for a very good reason. You would never forgive yourself if something went wrong because you weren't at the hospital. Less than three per cent of babies are born at home, so you haven't done anything wrong – you're merely totally normal!

You've 'succumbed' to pain relief you weren't planning to have

Only six per cent of women give birth without any pain relief at all. Why? Because giving birth is *bloody painful*. When you pop a paracetamol because you've got a headache, do you think you're being weak and pathetic? Of course not.

Childbirth is pretty heroic whether you did it on nothing more than positive thoughts or the full complement of drugs. And hey, you're a good girl who pays her taxes – why not make the most of it?

It's taking ages and ages and you're exhausted

Labour is the hardest work you'll ever do. Long labours are rubbish because they're so very tiring and you'll feel like it will never end. The important thing to remember is, it might not feel like it, but the end is near. Do whatever you need to do to make things more comfortable and start mentally composing your 'I was in labour for nine days' horror story for the parenting forums. And make yourself feel better by googling celebrities you dislike, with whom your baby will no longer share a birthday because you've run into the next day. Or the day after that.

You've got to have an emergency C-section

This is many mums' worst fear – or at least they think it is, until it happens, and then it's OK in the end. Whether it's the op itself or the recovery period you're fretting about, just remember: lots of mums actually *choose* to have caesareans – often more than once – so it can't be that bad, can it? And if you need one, it's because it's the best thing for you and your baby, and it's not something hospitals take lightly (not least because it costs them a lot more money). The biggest hurdle is often your pride, but talking to other C-section mums afterwards will help, as well as making sure your partner is aware that their postnatal responsibilities may have just stepped up a bit.

There's something wrong with the baby

The biggest source of freakoutery of all – and really the only one that matters a jot. Thankfully, it's also by far the least likely. There's nothing we can say to make you feel better if things go wrong, other than the obvious: everyone wants your baby to be OK, and they will do all they can to make sure it's the case. It's also important to remember that hospitals are very cautious, so even minor worries about your baby will be taken very seriously. But most issues will be just that: very minor indeed.

WHAT OUR MUM MATES SAY

If your baby is standing tall in your womb, refusing to turn around into the right position for birth but you've set yourself up for really wanting a natural birth, don't be disappointed when it all goes out of the window and you're advised to have a C-section. You honestly won't give a shit once the baby is born, you'll just care that it's healthy and fine. All the prep you get told you must do before, you don't have to do at all – it's all just a plot to distract you from the fact that you're going to somehow get a tiny human out of your body and it doesn't matter how . . . it's coming!

Julie, mum of one

No matter how well prepared you are – hypnobirthing classes, meditation, perineum massage (gulp!), a laminated birth plan (I didn't actually do this but my husband suggested it!), yoga – the perfect birth might not happen because: mother nature and biology. I was so adamantly anti-drugs and pro-natural labour that when every intervention known to man eventually happened, I felt crushed and a bit of a failure. Try not to get hung up on the idea of the perfect birth because it really doesn't matter how the baby gets here as long as you are safe and well.

Ru, mum of one

For my first birth I wanted – and was expecting – a really lovely, natural, drug-free, positive experience (our NCT lady advised us to make our partners a cake in labour, to 'thank for them for the beautiful gift' they had given us!). But it was an awful birth – 24 hours, failed forceps, episiotomy and Ventouse, baby born not crying and had to be resuscitated and so on. I was shell-shocked for ages afterwards and wish I'd been more open to the fact that birth could have gone either way. With my second, I didn't have a birth plan or any particular hopes or expectations other than we'd all make it out safely – which we did.

Maria, mum of two

One of my all-time favourite proverbs is an old Yiddish one: 'Man plans, God laughs'. Change 'man' to 'woman' and add the word 'birth' in before 'plans' and it's just as applicable. My advice would be to not have any expectations around the birth. The sheer concept of birth plans drives me up the frigging wall. I remember my midwife asking me to think about mine and I said '1) Take all the drugs and 2) pray it's shaped like a bullet.' She did not find it funny.

Manisha, mum of one

How to get the hell out of hospital

Congratulations, you did it! Isn't your baby amazing? Sure, sure, but what you really want now is your own bed, your own special, big chunky tea mug, plus lighting and heating and dinner options that you are in control of.

In the olden days – like when you were born – it was totally normal for mums to stay in hospital for upwards of a week, so that they would have support while they established feeding and recovered from childbirth. This is no longer the case and sounds bizarre to our modern, broadband-demanding selves, meaning that now, when you've given birth and your baby is all good, you'll be *desperate* to be sent home and you'll be expecting that to happen pretty soon. And, contrary to how you might feel, the hospital is actually keen to get rid of you too, since there's a whole production line of women in various stages of labour who have got dibs on your bed.

But it's not always as easy as that. There are a few things that need to happen before you'll be sent on your way. Often you're not warned about this, so you'll be feeling seriously impatient and might find yourself sitting on the edge of your hospital bed with your bags packed and your baby in the car seat way before you've been signed off. Here are a few things that will need to happen before you'll be allowed on your way.

1. Poo

Whatever kind of birth you've had, but particularly if you've had stitches 'down there', midwives will be fixated with your toilet habits. Basically, you won't be allowed to go home until you've managed to do a poo. And this kind of psychology isn't conducive to actually doing a poo, and nor is stodgy hospital food or the fact that you're sharing bathroom facilities with a number of noisy, knackered strangers. To help the process along, in the hours after giving birth try to drink lots of fluids, particularly fruit juice. And try to – ha – relax.

2. A well-fed baby

Breastfeeding can take time to get to grips with, and those midwives aren't going to set you free until they're confident that the baby is getting fed. Make the most of the feeding supporters in the hospital – ring that bell by your bed if you need their help and don't feel guilty; it's what they're there for. And it's *much* easier to ask for help now than at home, at 3.00 am, with a hungry baby squawking at your nipple.

3. Health checks

You thought your kid wouldn't have exams until they were at school, but during the first few hours of their lives, babies have a whole series of boxes to tick, from their reflexes to their hearing. Thanks to the strain on hospital staff, this can take time. Try to be a patient patient and just enjoy marvelling at this perfect creature you have created while you wait for the docs to do their rounds.

4. So. Much. Admin.

All of the above might be sorted in the morning – but it could still be the evening before you're allowed to actually leave, thanks to the staff being so damned busy that they haven't had time to fill in the relevant paperwork for you to get the hell out of there. Don't be afraid to nudge them, but always be polite – these people work verrrry hard and, like we said before, even though you are obviously sparkling company and their favourite inpatient of all time, they're as eager for you to leave as you are.

5. And then comes the fun bit ...

You thought you had the car seat sussed, but it turns out they're a whole lot more fiddly when there's a tiny, freshly hatched baby to contend with. Get your partner to lug the rest of your stuff to your ride first, and then deal with the small matter of the baby together. Words you'll hear many, many times over the coming weeks: *it gets easier*!

WHAT OUR MUM MATES SAY

Take stool softeners. Do not just pretend you'll never poo again. Eventually you will have to and after ten days of not, you'd rather give birth again, so do what you can to ease its, er, passage.

Eimear, mum of two

I struggled with breastfeeding for the first 24 hours – the combination of massive boobs and a sleepy 6lb baby was a tricky one to get to grips with. I just couldn't get into the right position and my nipple kept slipping out of his mouth without me realising. I got very stressed about this – I've always been someone who gets frustrated when they can't master things straight away, it was like trying to ride a bike aged four all over again – and burst into tears when a midwife said I wouldn't be able to go home until I'd cracked it, because I'd been in the hospital for four days and just wanted my own bed! In the end, another awesome, no-nonsense midwife managed to manhandle my boob firmly into my baby's mouth and it was all much easier from then on. Well, until we had to get the baby to the car in torrential rain, anyway ...

Bella, mum of two

3

The first six weeks

When everything is bonkers (but you won't even remember it in a year)

So, the hard bit's done. Right? Well, kind of. But what can happen at this point is that you'll suddenly realise you were so fixated on the whole giving birth thing that you didn't really think about what comes next: being a parent *for ever*. On a practical level, most first-timers are more than prepared for a baby invading their home, but what nobody can ever truly prepare for is the reality of caring for this tiny being whom you love so much that it physically hurts. Blend this all-new scary feeling with a load of hormonal madness, disrupted sleep and the practical challenges of all the new things you now need to master, from feeding to car seats, and it's fair to say that the first six weeks can be tough.

They're also really magical. When you look back in a few months' time, it will all just be a blur of cuddles and burps and that amazing newborn head smell, and you'll wonder why it all freaked you out so much. In the meantime, we hope we can reassure you that even the seemingly smuggest mums are just muddling through.

The A to Z of feeding your baby

It's one of the biggest conversation topics among new mums, mainly because you spend so much time doing it.

A is for appetite

Newborn babies feed *a lot*. At first you'll feel like you're in a relentless cycle of whipping your boob out and shoving it in their mouth and/or washing, sterilising and making up bottles. But it will settle in time and you'll probably be able to literally do it in your sleep.

B is for boobs or bottles, or both

Ah, the big one. We could write a whole book about the zillions of pros and cons of every feeding method. It is a flipping minefield. The basics: breastfeeding can be seriously tough at first, but becomes incredibly convenient after the first month or two. Bottle-feeding involves a lot more hauling stuff around, but means you can share the load with your partner. But it's not just about practicality: there are a whole world of emotional and physical things to think about too.

C is for colostrum

Otherwise known as liquid gold. It's the precious gunk that comes out of your boobs in the early days, before your more abundant milkier milk comes in. Many mums find themselves attempting to squeeze it into a syringe in hospital because their dozy baby is boob-resistant at first. Good times.

D is for dummies

Another minefield. Some mums swear by dummies from the start, some find they never need them and then secretly (or not so secretly) feel a bit smug about it when their friends then spend months trying to wean their toddlers off them. You can get Armani ones, you know. This world, eh?

E is for expressing

Otherwise known as pumping. You can get electric breast pumps (faster), manual breast pumps (quieter) and clever suction things that you can shove on one boob while feeding from the other (genius, if you can get the hang of it). Ignore anyone who likens you to a cow – or just focus on the fact that it must mean you have really great eyelashes. If you're a mum who pumps, you'll soon find yourself having to panic-eat fish fingers to make space in the freezer for your bulging supply. Excellent work!

F is for formula

There are various brands, but it's best to stick to one, since your baby's gut is sensitive, particularly in the early days. Lazy/loaded mums can buy the pre-made stuff – particularly handy for holidays and days out.

G is for grandparent

And older people in general. Some of them have some funny views about the way you feed your baby, wanting you to cover up excessively in public, for instance, or shove rusks in the bottom of bottles to fill your baby up (very bad idea). Nod, smile and instead speak to friends and professionals for more up-to-date insights.

H is for hands-free

We are always in awe of mums who stroll around without a care in the world while feeding their baby in a sling. Mainly because they must have really perky boobs.

I is for 'I can't do this!'

Most breastfeeding mums will have moments of feeling like this, especially in the early days. The best advice we've heard is that you should never quit on a bad day. See how you feel after a good night's sleep (ha!).

J is for judging

An unfortunate side effect of there being more than one way to feed your baby. But if you're a mum who's formula-feeding reluctantly after not getting on with the boob, or a breastfeeding mum who's carried on for much longer than expected (good for you!) and now feels a bit sheepish about it, you must remember that most, if not all, of the judging comes from only one person: you.

K is for kit

Bottle-feeding is definitely the more expensive option, especially when you start forking out for electric prep machines (one upstairs, one downstairs, anyone?), bottle warmers and ready-made formula, as well as the basics: powder, bottles and teats. But breastfeeding isn't without its costs too, especially if you want to pump, and especially if you get sucked into buying dedicated nursing clothes. (See O for more details.)

L is for leaking

Not all mums leak, so if you don't, it doesn't mean you have a poor supply. For most of us, it eases up after the first few weeks, and the breast pads can be relegated to the back of the cupboard (although they're pretty handy to have lying around for the seventeen spilled cups of tea per week). We'd also recommend keeping some on hand for when your baby starts sleeping for bigger chunks of time (it happens, we promise!) as you might find yourself waking up with two damp, swollen footballs bursting out of your bra.

M is for mastitis

Aaargh. We wouldn't wish it on our worst enemy. It's an inflammation of the boob that can cause flu-like symptoms and make you feel absolutely bloody rotten. Always see a doctor at the first signs because it can be – pun intended – nipped in the bud.

N is for Netflix

Or any other number of streaming services. Whichever way you're feeding your baby, on-tap quality entertainment is an essential in the early days. We have no idea what people used to do without them – crosswords and the *Emmerdale* omnibus?

O is for one up, one down

Often shortened on mum forums to OUOD, this is the easiest way to dress if you're breastfeeding: just wear a vest top you can pull down underneath a top you can pull up. Alternatively, vest tops you can pull up under low-cut/V-neck dresses you can pull down are also a winner. Basically, you don't really need loads of special breastfeeding clothes, and can easily improvise with your existing wardrobe and a few cheapo basics.

P is for pain

A bit of pain and discomfort is standard in the early days of feeding, as you and your baby get to grips with each other, but if you're experiencing pain that seems excessive, have a chat with your health visitor or a breastfeeding consultant, in case there are any underlying issues, such as a dodgy latch or tongue tie (see **T**).

Q is for quick

Feeding can take an age to start with, but as your baby grows, so does their capacity for guzzling milk at speed. It's quite a relief when you can fill them up in five minutes at a bus stop and go on with your day – although part of you will have emoshe pangs for the early days of endless feeding, no matter how much you moaned about it at the time.

R is for reflux

Bottle- and boob-fed babies can both suffer from reflux. In fact, it's very common in general and is often described as 'a laundry issue, not a medical issue'. A little bit is normal, but if it becomes a problem, you should speak to your doctor and rule out any allergies.

S is for support

Something you'll need lots of, especially if you're breastfeeding. There are fantastic NHS 'baby cafes' dotted around the country, where you can get advice on all aspects of feeding, numerous free helplines, as well as private lactation consultants who will pop round in a crisis (for a fee, naturally).

T is for tongue tie

A common condition in babies that often goes undiagnosed, but can make their feeding journey very tricky, despite being easy to fix. Always ask for a second opinion if you feel it's been overlooked.

U is for U R amazing

You are, you know! However you're feeding your precious offspring, it's draining, anxiety-causing stuff and you're doing a fantastic job of keeping them alive. They love U so much!

V is for vodka and vino

The research around drinking alcohol while breastfeeding is ongoing, but generally a couple of drinks won't do your baby any harm – professionals liken it to dropping a shot glass in an Olympic swimming pool. The bigger issue is around how safe you are to handle (and potentially sleep with) your baby when you've had a few drinks. 'Pumping and dumping' is also a myth – you don't need to throw away milk you make while drinking – it's not contaminated. But if you're away from your baby for an extended period of time, you might want to express for comfort.

W is for wind

Some people say that breastfed babies don't get wind. This is a big old lie. All babies get windy, especially in the early weeks, and you'll spend many hours rubbing their backs and googling 'tiger in the tree hold' (give it a go, it's pretty good). While technically the definition of 'colic' is 'excessive frequent crying', it's actually wind and the ensuing tummy pain that causes this – and it can be hellish. There are various potions, like Infacol and Gripe Water, that might ease the burps, but really the most successful cure is time: as your baby gets older and bigger, they'll get way more efficient at digesting their milk.

X is for XXL

This is how big your boobs will feel – relative to how big they normally are, anyway – on day four or five, when your milk comes in. It can come as quite a shock if you're normally a member of the itty bitty titty committee. Make sure you immortalise this moment on film before your baby guzzles the lot (and you can show it to your plastic surgeon in a couple of years, right?).

Y is for yoga

Or yoga-esque moves, anyway. As you learn your way around your baby, you'll find yourself contorting into all sorts of strange positions to feed them. The cradle hold, the rugby hold, the koala hold, biological nurturing ... yep, these all exist and they all work differently on different mums, depending on the shape of your body, the type of boobs you have (lovely ones, obvs) and the size of your baby. Remember, there's no 'wrong' way of doing it – you'll soon find a technique that works for you.

Z is for Zzzzzz

Ahh, precious sleep. Remember that? While breastfed babies generally feed more frequently in the night than their formula-fed buddies (because formula is harder to digest and so keeps babies fuller for longer), there's evidence to suggest that boobing mums get better quality sleep – partly because they're not getting out of bed to make up bottles, and partly because breastfeeding releases some clever hormones to aid sleep in both you and your baby. It's all by the by though, since we know the truth: *all* mums long for more sleep!

WHAT OUR MUM MATES SAY

I swear that video they show in antenatal classes of a baby just instinctively wriggling up its mum's body and latching onto her boob must be pure CGI – I don't know anyone who found it that easy! The mums I know who got on best with breastfeeding just accepted that the first few weeks were going to be hard and sought out support. I'm glad I stuck at it because I couldn't bear the thought of faffing around with bottles in the middle of the night.

Marie, mum of two

I chose not to breastfeed and it sounds silly but at times it felt like the most controversial decision I'd ever made! But I knew it was the right decision for my mental health, and that my mental health would affect the baby way more than what kind of milk she was drinking.

Laura, mum of one

The hardest part of breastfeeding for me was trying to find time to express as well. I was determined to have a stash of milk so that I could have a bit of freedom and share some of the feeds with my husband, but it was easier said than done. The pump worked so slowly compared to feeding plus my baby was feeding so much in the early days that there was just no time for it. And by the time the feeds had got more spread out, he wouldn't take a bottle anymore! I have huge respect for mums who manage to pump.

Abby, mum of one

Your name's not down, you're not coming in – what to do with the endless stream of visitors

So, you've made it home. Finally! But ... why is there a queue of people outside your house/clogging up your WhatsApp, just desperate to meet your precious firstborn?

Of course, you want your loved ones to gaze at your perfect creation in wonder. But you're also knackered, keen to get settled and adapt to life as a mum, without worrying about whether you've got enough milk in the fridge to serve tea to seven clucking aunties, twelve broody mates and one awkward father-in-law who's looking everywhere except at your swollen boobs.

Every mum we've met says she regrets allowing quite so many visitors round in those early weeks with a newborn. While you're getting to grips with looking after a baby and all it entails, and trying to enjoy your first days as a family while your partner has time off, you need a bit of space. There are some people who'll naturally require and (hopefully!) deserve priority access to your babe – grandparents and your bestest friend in the whole wide world, for instance – but the rest, with a bit of careful management, can wait. Here are a few tips to keep everyone happy – including you.

1. Operate strict timeslots

Visitors are inevitable – but they needn't hang around all day. It's hard to turf people out if they pop round on a Sunday lunchtime, but inviting them over in the evening means you can legitimately restrict their visit without looking rude. If they come round at 7.00 pm, you can totally say you're going up to bed at 9.00 pm. See ya! It also means you can spend daytimes *en famille*, and might even be grateful for the extra company in the evening (especially if they bring food).

2. Avoid visits on days four and five

A few days after you give birth, your milk comes in and your hormones go haywire and you might cry. A lot. And want to eat chocolate. A lot. And definitely not get out of your pyjamas. At all. This is *totally normal* but is not a time that you will want to be sociable. Spend it nesting with your partner and shiny new baby and, hopefully, come out the other side feeling slightly less delicate. Also, make sure your partner is aware of the existence of the baby blues, so they don't just think you're being a diva.

3. Force people to be useful

Now is the time to make the most of people's goodwill. If you're (either begrudgingly or happily) expecting company, for God's sake don't let them turn up empty-handed. If they say 'Anything you'd like me to bring?' don't say 'Just your lovely self!' Instead suggest they pick up a takeaway, or whatever else you fancy. If they're a close enough friend or relative that they've been granted early days access, they won't be offended. And when they arrive, don't rush around after them, offering drinks – they can jolly well take the initiative and help their flipping selves.

4. Consider a group event

It's not for the faint-hearted, but there's a lot to be said for getting it over with in one go. OK, so you might not feel much like party-planning, but inviting one group of friends, or one side of the family, over en masse on, say, a Saturday afternoon, will free up the rest of your time. This is especially appealing if you've birthed a summer baby, as they can hang out in the garden rather than cluttering up your house. If you have lots of people over at once, it's also easier to inconspicuously slip upstairs with the baby when you need a breather – less possible when you have one visitor firing questions at you about your postnatal blood flow.

5. Learn to say no

You're a mum now, and mums are flaky. Over the coming months, you'll plan and cancel more outings than you thought possible, because babies have an annoying habit of sometimes being a bit socially uncooperative. If you've said yes to some visitors but now don't feel up to it, for whatever reason, just be honest with them. If they don't get it now, one day they probably will. Likewise, it's OK to say no to your baby being randomly handed around the room. It's *your* baby and you're quite entitled to want to hold onto them (although it's also totally OK if you're fine with playing pass the pooey parcel and take the opportunity for a well-earned breather/sip of your tea while it's still hot).

6. Leave the book open on this page close to the focal point of the room (i.e. your baby)

Your visitors will soon get the hint. Hiya Auntie Pam, looking fab, have you done something different with your hair? Thanks for the fluffy bunny comforter ... now be off with you.

WHAT OUR MUM MATES SAY

I was totally overwhelmed by the amount of visitors we had during the first month or so, but felt like I couldn't say no. I remember one weekend we had six different groups at different times – except some turned up late and others early, so it was chaos. It was exhausting and I didn't feel like we had any downtime together as a family. Second time I planned to be much stricter, but actually it wasn't as much of an issue because nobody's as interested in your second child anyway!

Mary, mum of two

I used to glare at even good friends coming round and holding my baby. They weren't doing it right! You are allowed to be totally irrational at this stage and feel like only you know how.

Katie, mum of two

How to look after yourself when it's all about the baby

Hey, remember you? That whole person who existed before the baby came along? When you're in the thick of it, it's really tricky to prioritise your own needs and desires. But a little bit of self-care can go a long way when it comes to maintaining your sanity and self-esteem.

Don't neglect your wounds

If you had stitches or an episiotomy, you're going to need to take care of 'it'. In fact, however you gave birth, you're going to need to take care of 'it'. Just sloping around the house can make you sore in the early days after giving birth – and if you're one of the really lucky ones, you might even find yourself suffering from haemorrhoids (seriously, haven't you been through enough?) – so use painkillers if you need to, change your pad regularly and try to find time for nice soothing baths (your baby can always join you). Your bits will be checked over at your six- to eight-week check, but any more pressing concerns should be flagged up with your GP or health visitor before that.

Go to bed early

Easier said than done when your baby is a long way off having any kind of routine, but take advantage of the little window of opportunity that might arise when your partner gets in from work. Make sure your baby is well-fed, pass them your partner's way for some nice, early-evening bonding and just lie the hell down. Even if you don't have a proper sleep and your baby is squawking for yet another feed within half an hour, the rest will do you good.

Squeeze in a shower

You'll feel way better about everything if you're clean. If you have the energy, jump in the shower first thing before your partner goes to work. Otherwise, that aforementioned window when they get home is a good opportunity for a quick spritz (you can lie down afterwards and revel in your delicious cleanness). Don't panic though, you'll soon suss out a way to shower when it's just you and your baby. Bouncy chairs and cot mobiles can be a godsend!

Get some air

If you've got a C-section scar or painful stitches, or if you've had a winter baby and it's vile outside, or, indeed, you're in the middle of a scorching heatwave, it can be tempting to just hole up at home in the early weeks. But getting a bit of fresh air is crucial for your well-being. If you can get to grips with a baby carrier early on, it's way less faff than having to lug the pram down the road for a five-minute stroll.

Eat proper meals

If you were super-organised in the later stages of pregnancy and now have a freezer full of chillis and pies and pasta bakes to work your way through, you'll now be reaping the benefits. But if you weren't quite this organised because you naively preferred sitting round watching box sets and cooing over pictures of baby clothes, you might need to enlist a bit of help now. Take advantage of any kindly relatives or neighbours bearing casserole dishes (even if it means you have to let them have a quick cuddle with your baby) and make sure your fruit bowl is as well stocked as your biscuit tin.

Give yourself a little treat

Use those tiny windows of freedom to your advantage – shave your armpits! Paint your toenails! Pluck your eyebrows! It's all about the micro-treats, even if you used to just think of them as basic bodily upkeep rather than pampering exercises. It doesn't have to be physical stuff either, of course – watching your favourite film with your baby asleep on your chest will also get those warm and fuzzy feelings flowing.

WHAT OUR MUM MATES SAY

A sports water bottle filled with warm water and a drop of tea tree oil is magic on your poor bits during post-Labour wees.

Ru, mum of one

I can't function without a shower in the morning, so I knew I had to make it work somehow. To start with, I'd try to jump in before my husband left the house, but this felt a bit frantic, so I quickly developed a routine of popping my baby in his cot with his jungle cot mobile whirring while I had a quick shower. His room is next to the bathroom so I left the door open and could hear any whimpers. I didn't often manage to properly wash my hair, but just feeling clean was enough to make me feel more sane.

Izzy, mum of two

Five things to do when you're trapped on the sofa feeding

Newsflash: newborn babies don't do very much. And most of what they do happens on or around your body. This means you're about to spend more time than you ever imagined sitting and/or lying down, tending to your baby's every feeding/sleeping/pooing need.

On some levels, especially if you're quite lazy, this is

blissful. In the olden days – and it's still the case in some cultures – new mums were encouraged to hibernate for the first few weeks, or even months, with a baby, while getting waited on by extended family/maternity nurses. These days, we tend to acknowledge that fresh air and social interaction are quite important for our sanity, plus everyone's too busy to be so hands-on anyway – and who can afford a maternity nurse? But don't underestimate the value of the sofa weeks. In fact, make the most of them. You'll roll your eyes when people bleat clichés like 'They're not tiny for long! You won't get this time again!' but seriously, *it is the truth*!

1. Go box-set crazy

A streaming subscription is the greatest gift a new mum can get. Give it a few months, and your baby won't let you watch telly (unless it's CBeebies). You'll also start worrying about them overhearing rude words/catching a glimpse of Jon Hamm's bare bum, so now is the time to watch whatever you want to watch, whenever you want to watch it. Want a trashy, high school drama fix at 4.00 am? Go for it! No need to feel guilty – you're busy sustaining life.

2. Do the shopping

Taking your newborn to the supermarket can be a fun challenge, as you enter a mysterious new world of trollies with different kinds of baby seats and trying to get a baby out of a car seat when all the family spaces have been taken up by selfish childless *criminals*. But the challenge can wait. For now, revel in being able to get the weekly shop done, on your phone, while there's a baby attached to your boob. And when it arrives and there are seventeen packets of biscuits? It's not your fault – you ordered one-handed and mistakes happen. Right?

3. Catch up on your correspondence

OK, we're not suggesting you'll have the energy to write proper thank-you letters, but there are plenty of sites and apps around that allow you to make custom-made thank-you cards, so order now and get round to sending them later. Much later. Also, a good excuse to trawl through the seven zillion pictures you've already taken of your baby to find the one that best says 'I might *look* sleepy and a bit like an expressionless old man/alien hybrid but I appreciate your gift from the bottom of my heart.'

4. Exercise

Haha. We're not talking actual workouts – those can wait (perhaps a very long time), but now is a most excellent time to tend to your poor pelvic floor. And then congratulate yourself with a bit more sitting down.

5. Absolutely nothing

All of the above is optional. It's perfectly fine if all you want to do right now is gaze at the amazing creature you have created, and memorise every millimetre of his or her perfect little face. And you can definitely do this while eating. This is also an optimum time for 'you and baby' selfies – all those love hormones floating around mean that, even though you're knackered and shell-shocked, you're all gooey-eyed and gorgeous, despite #nofilter. Make the most of it!

WHAT OUR MUM MATES SAY

During a sofa day, I blearily got some lovely cards printed up through one of those dead simple card-making apps to thank everyone for the presents they'd sent. They had a really cute picture of my little boy on the front and a nice blank space on the back for writing on ... or so I thought until the cards actually arrived a few days later. In my sleep-deprived state, I hadn't noticed that there was default text on there which I was supposed to edit ... so I ended up with 40 cards printed with the words 'Introducing the light of our lives, Emilia'. Emilia's a beautiful name, but it was very much not his. I debated whether to cross it out, stick something over it or just roll with the joke, but in the end I just never got round to sending them. Nearly three years on, thanks for the presents, everyone!'

Izzy, mum of two

I happened to hear a midwife on the radio talking about how she recommends a week in bed, then a week on the sofa for every new mum. That sounds like good advice to me! Even though we were out and about doing stuff quite early on, I think the advice of staying horizontal for the majority of the first couple of weeks would have done me good. I was lucky that my husband didn't need to be told to do everything – I don't think I changed a nappy in the first two weeks; all I did was the breastfeeding, he did all the rest, including bringing me endless snacks and cups of tea!

Jess, mum of one

What to chuck in your changing bag

During the third trimester, you'll waste many hours packing, emptying and repacking your shiny new changing bag. Then, in the early weeks, you'll empty it all out and start again. Nappies, wipes, nappy bags, nipple pads and a change of clothes for baby are pretty obvious, but what else could you find yourself needing the first time you dare to leave the house?

Barrier cream

It's crazy how much newborns manage to poo. Plus, they sometimes do stealth poos that you don't notice straight away, both of which mean they're prone to nappy rash, which is no fun for anyone. Arm yourself with nappy cream at all times. The little weeny sample pots are super-handy if you can find one.

A soft book

You might not think your baby will care about toys and books when they're tiny, but actually, most seem to enjoy bright, tactile distractions from the word go. A soft book squashes down small enough to keep in your changing bag and can be whipped out in times of need.

So. Many. Muslins

If you've got a pukey baby, it's true that you can never have enough muslins. But that's not their only purpose. They're handy to cover up when breastfeeding (soon you won't give a monkey's who sees your boobs, but to start with you might feel nervous about whacking them out), to pop on the ground if you find yourself changing a nappy in the park – and this *will* happen – and to mop up the various spillages you'll cause when you try to hold a baby and sip a drink at the same time.

Hand sanitiser

Those nappies you'll inevitably change on the hoof can make you feel a bit grubby. Wet wipes are a godsend, but hand sanitiser will make you feel extra hygienic, even if you haven't managed to shower for three days.

Snacks for you

If you're breastfeeding, you'll be hungry roughly every three minutes. And if you're not, you'll still be hungry every three minutes because this baby-rearing business is tiring. Make sure you've always got a stash of easy-to-eat snacks in your change bag (flapjacks or dried fruit are both good options) to avoid hangry meltdowns when your baby has pinned you to a bench because it's decided now is a good time to feed/sleep.

Nipple cream

If you've got sore boobs out and about, you'll want to have your lanolin cream on standby. It's not cheap and you don't want to have to buy more if you can avoid it, so keep a tube in your bag for nippular crises. Turns out, it also makes a pretty good lip balm.

WHAT OUR MUM MATES SAY

With my first, I carried a little bottle of cooled boiled water along with some cotton wool in my changing bag for weeks, because I didn't want to compromise his precious bum! Needless to say, with number two I went straight for the wipes. Life's too short for cooled boiled water!

Lucy, mum of two

I carried a lightweight scarf to start with – it hides a multitude of stains, nipple flashing and can be used as a sick wipe! I also always had some nice lip balm in my bag – it can't all be for the baby ...

Katie, mum of two

Five things every new mum worries about – and why you shouldn't

Ugggggh. Thanks to hormones, sleep deprivation and that crazy all-consuming love, newborns don't half make us worry. No matter how much of a chilled-out entertainer you usually are, in those first few weeks of motherhood, it's totally, utterly normal to find yourself fretting about all sorts of things that your pre-mum self would roll her eyes at.

This list could have touched on at least eighty-seven different worries but these are the big ones, the concerns that have every mum of a newborn asking strangers on the internet really specific questions at four in the morning.

1. 'The baby is too hot! The baby is too cold!'

When you first bring your baby home, irrational concerns about their body temperature will plague you. Baby born in a heatwave? You'll still find yourself faffing around with layers and blankets.

Always remind yourself that your baby is a human being, not a weird otherworldly creature who experiences their environment completely differently from you, and that there are babies thriving around the world in all sorts of weather conditions.

If you're a bit hot, they're probably a bit hot too. If you're a bit cold, they're probably a bit cold too. Feel the temperature of their chest and adjust their layers accordingly, just as you would with your own. It's not an exact science. And the whole 'they should wear one more layer than you' thing that everyone bleats at you is a mere guide. Use your common sense, which can be reclaimed down the back of the changing table, under a sick-scented muslin and some discarded breast pads.

2. 'They're feeding too much!'

If you're breastfeeding, this will drive you mad. You'll feel like you're feeding *constantly* (especially if you have one of those babies that likes to fall asleep on the boob – that's all of them, then). New mums often write down all of their babies' bodily functions but this really isn't necessary.

The fact is, babies – especially those on the smaller side – feed loads as a cunning way of building up your milk supply, and the advice about newborns only feeding every four hours is outdated and potentially dangerous. Just follow their lead – they're clever little things – and as long as they're gaining weight and filling nappies, it's all good. When they're older and won't stay still, you'll yearn for those long, cosy days on the sofa, trying to reach the remote with your toe.

3. 'They're sleeping too much! They're not sleeping enough!'

We've all got that mum friend who seemingly faux-moans about their baby sleeping too much, and you'll feel like screaming *'Good for you!'* as you calculate that you've had eleven hours sleep in two weeks.

When babies are tiny, sleeping too much is only a concern if they're jaundiced and/or not gaining weight quickly. And as for not sleeping enough ... it's mainly because they hate you. Or, you know, *they're a baby*. Just remember, they'll sort themselves out one day. Probably about a week before you get pregnant again.

4. 'Their poo looks weird'

We hate to break it to you but *your* poo looks weird some-times too. There's a wide range of normalness when it comes to baby poo – googling it is a bit like a gross version of a Dulux colour chart – but if you're really worried, you can mention it to your health visitor, who will have heard, seen and smelled it all before.

Weird poo without other symptoms is generally nothing to worry about. And trust us when we say that runny, new-born poo in all its shades of yellow, orange and green is *way* less gross than what comes when they start on solids. All in good time ...

5. 'Why do they look so gross?'

We can blame nappy adverts and Instagram filters for this. Turns out real newborns don't all have soft, flawless skin. They all have phases of being spotty, flaky, wrinkly and/or red. It's totally normal and a result of living in the luxurious confines of your body for so long.

Always get proper rashes checked out, but the zits and the flakiness are generally just a brief, unphotogenic preview of adolescence and old age.

WHAT OUR MUM MATES SAY

Our friends took their lovely chubby baby out for the day. When they got home, they noticed his legs looked weird – discoloured and with a rash on them. They rushed to hospital, convinced he had meningitis, but it turned out that the baby carrier they had squeezed him into was too tight on his plump little legs, and had cut off the circulation.

Saskia, mum of one

We were worried when our daughter was unresponsive and floppy at a few weeks old. We rang the doctor and they asked us to try really hard to get a response so we poked her and shook her gently by the shoulders. She didn't wake up and they said they were sending an ambulance and we were to try everything we could to get a response from the baby. Having been reasonably calm until now, I suddenly panicked and threw a glass of water on her. Baby woke up. Very very angry. 'Sorry,' we said to the doctor over the screams, 'it seems she was asleep.'

Helen, mum of one

Our first unnecessary trip to A&E – not our last! – was the most neurotic ... my little boy swallowed some water during baby swimming class. He was extra sleepy (I thought) later on and I convinced myself he had water on his lungs and was secondary drowning (I'd seen a scaremongering Facebook post a week or so before). He was obviously *totally fine*. Needless to say, we weren't top of the list at A&E.

Lucy, mum of two

The six (million) stages of leaving the house with a newborn

How hard can it be to get a tiny creature out of the house on time? *Really flipping hard*, it transpires.

Stage One: Getting ready

If you don't manage to get a shower in while your partner is still at home in the morning, you have two choices: a) Manoeuvring something – bouncy chair, changing mat, Moses basket are all options, space permitting – into your bathroom and hoping your baby will tolerate lolling in it long enough for you to spritz yourself with water. Or b) Stink.

Both are acceptable at this stage in the game. Either way, you then need to get yourself dressed, by grabbing the nearest cleanish clothes you can find. Ten thousand bonus smug points to you if you locate matching socks.

Stage Two: Getting the baby ready

The first part involves looking out of the window at the weather or, if you're trapped under a baby and the curtains are shut, checking the weather forecast on your phone. You can then dress your baby. Maybe you have one of those chilled-out babies who takes nappy changes and the wriggling-on of leggings in their stride, or maybe you're now going to get kicked in the face and screamed at. Either way, this shouldn't take too, too long, depending on the current contents of their nappy.

Stage Three: Sustenance

Breakfast is the most important meal of the day, they say, but when you're a new mum, specific mealtimes are kind of fluid. Multi-tasking mums like to balance a cereal bowl on their baby's body while their boob is in action but we wouldn't recommend this unless you like spilled cereal and angry babies. Toast, pastries or cereal bars are an easier on-the-move/on-the-boob option (and always choose a buggy you can drag around one-handed so that your other hand can accommodate toast – there's no shame in it).

The problem is, post-feed, there's now a strong possibility that your baby will fall asleep, ruining your best-laid plans. If you're heading out with a buggy or sling, a stealth transfer can be attempted, but this is trickier if you need to try to get a coat or other layers onto them first.

Stage Four: Packing

Whether you use a traditional changing bag or just shove items haphazardly into a rucksack or carrier bag, this part involves brain power. You will, of course, always forget something. At first, this will feel catastrophic but, remember, most things are available in the – whisper it – outside world. Becoming a mum is also great for your improvisation skills. Many things can double up as mislaid baby wipes. Including your clothes.

Stage Five: Actually leaving the house

You're dressed, you're packed, you're good to go. Doesn't it feel amazing? Almost as amazing as the sweet, sweet smell of newborn poo that's oozing from your baby ... back to Stage Two.

Stage Six: Actually leaving the house

Quick, run before something else happens! And also, because you're now really, really late. Sounds stressful? It can be, but it's important to remember two things: a) It. Gets. Easier. b) You will always, *always* feel better for leaving the house, so try not to give up halfway through. Fresh air and human interaction are the most important things for a new mum.*

WHAT OUR MUM MATES SAY

The first time I went on public transport with my little girl, we crammed our way onto one of those neighbours-in-armpits buses. She was fast asleep in the sling, which I felt quite smug about, but then she had the mother of all poos. It was incredibly loud, and if that didn't catch the attention of the entire bus, the sweet smell of newborn baby poo definitely did as it spread through the air – and all down her legs.

Saskia, mum of one

---

* Well, after chocolate and sleep.

On our first day out of the hospital post C-section, we went for a walk. I had to sit on a wall to rest, which happened to be near some teenagers playing volleyball. I passed the baby to my husband and then got whacked in the face by a volleyball, bit my own tongue, burst into tears and got shouted at by a man who said I shouldn't be there if I had just had a baby. It definitely got easier after that.

Julie, mum of one

Getting out of the house in one piece was a challenge at the start. I dropped and broke my phone so many times due to frantically trying to look up the addresses of classes and feeding support groups while trying to push my pram at the same time! My phone insurance excess is not pretty as a result but it was great to get out of the house and talk to other mums – mainly about sleep!

Kate, mum of one

I left the front door wide open for four hours the first time I ventured out alone with the baby. Amazingly, we weren't burgled!

Emily, mum of two

What to do if you're feeling blue

It's normal to go through some pretty major highs and lows when you've just had a baby. This is the biggest change in your life in the entire history of *ever*, so of course your mind, body and soul are going to take a beating. Even though we know it's all worth it in the end, it doesn't make it any easier at the time.

According to the NHS, around ten per cent of women experience mental health issues after having a baby – and actually, the real figure is likely to be far higher, since many new mums don't seek professional help, putting the way they're feeling down to tiredness and hormones. It's not just depression and anxiety that can affect new mums, but also post-traumatic stress (especially if you've had a particularly rough birth), postnatal psychosis and tokophobia: fear of pregnancy and childbirth. While these conditions aren't as common, they do happen.

We're told that having a baby is the most wonderful thing in the world, so when it feels so hard, overwhelming and emotionally fraught, we can be afraid to speak out – or we're just so frazzled and busy looking after our newborn that we're unable to prioritise hauling our exhausted asses to the doctor's.

There are a few red flags that could suggest you're going through more than just the 'baby blues' – here's what to look out for.

You're exhausted, but you can't sleep

'Sleep while the baby sleeps' is one of the most annoying clichés new mums hear. If only it was so easy, eh? Particularly when you have an endless flow of visitors to entertain *and* a laundry basket full of seemingly multiplying baby socks.

But if, even when you're tucked up in bed, you still find

yourself struggling to switch off and get your head down, or if you're suffering from vivid nightmares, it could be a symptom of PND or PTSD.

The best thing you can do is talk to people – your partner, family, friends. It can be hard to let go in the early days, but letting someone else take responsibility for your baby for just a couple of hours while you rest can make the difference between short-term knackeredness and long-term mental health issues. Even if you don't sleep, just opening up and taking a bit of time out will help you feel less overwhelmed and give you the chance to reflect on how you're really feeling.

Your eating habits have changed

It's extremely challenging to eat a well-balanced diet when you've just had a baby, when your normal routine has gone out of the window ... plus every new mum deserves a Hobnob or three.

But eating habits and mental health are hugely intertwined, with many people either comfort eating or, at the opposite end of the scale, experiencing loss of appetite when they're depressed or anxious.

If your partner is taking charge of food during the early days, they might not be prioritising healthy eating either, since they're also likely to be feeling pretty frazzled, but hopefully talking to them will help. And never be afraid to mention it to your health visitor or doctor too. Self-care is tough when you're putting all your energy into your baby, but it's important for you *and* them that you're as strong and healthy as possible.

You're withdrawing from your friends

This can be a tough one to spot when you're the one doing it. If you've got a gaggle of mum friends who get together en masse, it can be hard to have a proper chat – conversation threads are often left unfinished due to badly-timed baby meltdowns or unexpected nappy incidents.

Less outgoing personalities can also find themselves drowned out by all the chatter. If this is you, it doesn't necessarily mean you're depressed. But if you have been feeling a bit down, talking to friends in a similar frame of mind could nip any more serious issues in the bud. If you feel like chatting properly would help, but struggle to get heard in a crowd, try to arrange one-on-one meet-ups.

You're really anxious about your baby

It's totally normal to worry about everything – from your newborn's body temperature to the colour of their poo – but, in mums suffering from PND and/or anxiety, these concerns can be heightened to the point that they're crippling. This can lead to being scared to do things that wouldn't normally bother you, such as taking your little one out to the shops.

A good health visitor or doctor (or indeed your partner) should be able to spot signs that you're overly obsessing about your baby's well-being. What you really need is reassurance that you're a wonderful, caring mum and the acceptance that *everyone* finds it scary to suddenly be responsible for a tiny human.

Once again, the best thing you can do is talk, talk, talk. Because you're not the only one feeling like this. Lots of mums put on their 'happy face' at baby groups for fear of being judged or labelled a bad mum if they share their true worries and fears. The more we talk openly and honestly about our mental health, the more chance we have of getting support. And did we mention what a bloody brilliant job you're doing?

WHAT OUR MUM MATES SAY

I had a relatively traumatic labour and my baby was tube fed for the first few days. I know many people successfully breastfeed after this, and I was in a special unit to help establish it, but it wasn't happening, and I felt defeated and totally bewildered. It really affected bonding and when I came home from hospital I resented my husband for being able to bottle feed her – we even had a blazing row because I felt like he was attending to her without giving me a chance. I felt myself slipping down a horrible spiral of resentment and it was only when one of my new mum friends said it was OK to use formula that something just clicked and I began to enjoy my baby. I think if I had carried on with the endless feed-pump-feed-sleep schedule I would have suffered serious PND.

Ru, mum of one

Don't worry if you're not overwhelmed with love for the new baby. With my first I was expecting a surge but after a traumatic labour I was totally numb. The love developed very gradually over the first few weeks. I now know that this was pretty normal but at the time I was worried I was some sort of freak.

Beth, mum of two

On the telly people seem to always talk about having an instant bond with your baby, but to be honest it took me a few weeks. I was almost a bit scared of this strange new creature that had taken over my life. I was so sleep deprived I would occasionally fantasise that someone was coming to take her away from me. It feels strange saying this now, but during those first weeks I was totally discombobulated.

Sarah, mum of two

Five maddening clichés you'll hear five thousand times in the first few weeks (months, years)

As if your body hadn't been through enough, you've now got to bite your tongue as well. Why? Because you're about to hear the same old clichés over and over again from (mostly) well-meaning friends, relatives and total strangers. Er, some of them might have snuck into this very book as well. Here are the big ones – and the truth.

1. 'It gets easier'

Is it true? Yes! Mostly. There's nothing like the shellshock of the early days with an alien newborn, but babies do eventually learn the difference between night and day and they won't always feed what feels like every twelve seconds. That said, there will always be ups and downs – teething, sleep regressions, illness and just annoying rainy days can all make you feel rubbish – but the fun you'll have and the love you'll feel will take the edge off. So, yes, it *does* get easier. You're not being tricked.

2. 'You must sleep while the baby sleeps'

Is it true? In theory, it's a genius idea. But when the words come from a relative who is in your house, drinking your coffee and chewing your ear off, all while your baby is dozing away, you'll feel a bit murderous and they won't quite see the irony. There's also the fact that sleeping while the baby sleeps is considerably harder if your baby will only sleep on you.

3. 'It's just a phase'

Is it true? Kind of. Your baby will indeed have phases of sleeping badly, sleeping well, being a little angel and being a total douchebag, for instance, but while you're in the thick of them, being told 'it's just a phase' will annoy you. Because it doesn't make it any easier, does it? Especially when said cliché-spouter cannot give you the exact date this so-called phase will end. Remember though, guys, it gets easier!

4. 'You'll never finish a hot drink'

Is it true? Not necessarily. It depends how much you like hot drinks – if you are a total caffeine addict you'll always prioritise gulping down your beverage of choice before tending to your baby's nappy. So fear not: a life of grim, lukewarm refreshments in mugs ringed with stains of the many unfinished drinks before them does not necessarily await. It's all about your priorities.

5. 'It goes so fast'

Is it true? God, yes! At least, eventually. While pregnancy feels like an age, motherhood can race along. It's strange really, because some days – especially in the first couple of months – have a habit of dragging so much you'll feel like you're wading through treacle (the minutes between 4.00 and 6.00 pm will sometimes feel like decades), but then you won't believe that you suddenly have a twelve-week-old, and then a six-month-old, and then – sob! – an actual adult human leaving home to start a life of their own. Woah, now you're a granny!

WHAT OUR MUM MATES SAY

I found it really hard when people said 'It goes by in a flash!' because I found the first year really dragged by and it made me feel like I was doing it wrong and not savouring my time with my baby enough. Now that my eldest is at school, I look back and think 'Wow, that *was* fast' so

I get where they are coming from, but it wasn't helpful when I felt like I was spending every day counting down the hours until bedtime!

*Nicky, **mum of two***

My mum loves telling me that things are just a phase – in fact, she's done it all my life, not just in relation to my baby! I know it is well-meaning and she's trying to make the point that the bad sleep or the fussy eating or whatever will improve soon, but all I want to do is scream in her face *'If it's just a phase then tell me when it will be over!'* But it's best to just nod and smile …

*Izzy, **mum of two***

Things that will happen the first time you take your baby to the supermarket

Your local, soulless chain supermarket is quite likely to be the destination of one of your first solo trips with the baby. But what will happen once you're there?

1. You will freak out about trolleys

In your pre-baby life, you would swan around the supermarket with one of those nice, lightweight, shallow trolleys, or maybe even just a basket, which would be efficiently filled with wine and nice fish, and whichever shampoo and conditioner was on 2-for-1. Now those days (the ones where you regularly washed your hair) are over. You need a mammoth trolley and you need to pile it high with nappies and chocolate.

But how on earth do you cart this *and* a newborn around? This dilemma will plague you. You'll message your mum mates about it and google it late at night. You basically have three options: a) Baby in sling plus normal trolley, b) Baby in car seat in normal (big) trolley or c) Trolley with special little baby seat in it. (These are like gold dust, but put on your best 'clueless new mum face' to ask a nice member of staff and one might magically appear.)

And something to look forward to: in a few months, when your tiny squish has learned to sit up, this all gets a *lot* easier, as you can just plonk them in a standard trolley with child seat, of which there are zillions.

2. You will feel irrationally guilty about claiming a parent and child parking space

How your childless self longed to park in the best seats in the house. Now you have a legit reason to, but you'll still feel a bit guilty about it. You'll make sure your baby on board sign is very prominently displayed and make a big thing out of getting your baby out of the car (to be fair, it *is* a big thing right now ... soon it will be second nature). Relax – the space is yours and nobody thinks you're a great big faker. Own it.

3. You will get distracted by baby clothes

You went in for washing detergent, wipes and teabags, and yet you find yourself leaving with all of the above *and* a pile of irresistible baby clothes. Supermarket baby swag is excellent value and there's no spending guilt, since if it can be bought at a supermarket, then it *must* be a baby essential, right? Go crazy for those multipacks of colourful vests – this is how you get your kicks now.

4. A clucky old lady will make everything better

One of your main worries about supermarket shopping with a small person is that your fellow shoppers will hate you. This couldn't be further from the truth – you're a daytime person now, and your fellow daytime people are mostly pretty baby-friendly. Your newborn will get cooed over in the veg aisle by a gaggle of pensioners and make you feel way more at ease, so much so that you'll wonder if Tesco hires undercover clucky old ladies for this very purpose.

5. You will get into a bit of a kerfuffle

At some point, something annoying will happen. Perhaps you've got the baby in a sling but now can't reach the high shelves. Perhaps you need a wee but can't work out how to do that with a trolley full of shopping and a newborn. Perhaps there's been a poonami in aisle twelve.

Life with a newborn is rarely straightforward but, rest assured, these things happen to all mums, all the time, and they're never as traumatic as you imagine them to be. And supermarkets are the best place you can be – they sell everything you could possibly need for every crisis, there are friendly people everywhere and you can reward yourself with a hot drink and some cake at the end of it.

6. Sorry, but, at some point, your baby will cry

Babies are often good as gold as you work your way around the aisles, enjoying the motion of the trolley and the noise and bright colours, but then freak out when you get to the check-out, i.e. the worst possible time, because you have actual time-sensitive tasks to carry out.

Don't panic – nobody goes to the supermarket for the quiet, chilled-out vibes and, in the course of a normal day, the staff will have served dozens of stressed parents of squawking children of all sizes. Just grin and bear it and make the most of the fact that somebody will probably now swiftly appear to help you with your packing and get you out of there – not because they hate you, but because they empathise.

7. You'll fantasise about doing this alone

What used to be a chore now becomes your deepest darkest fantasy – imagine being able to do this *by yourself*. Think of the time you could spend perusing mid-range shower gels if only you were unencumbered by a small child. In the near future, this day will come – doing the shop while your partner does bedtime may well become your Friday night out, and it will feel *amazing*. Something to look forward to, eh? It's coming, we promise ...

WHAT OUR MUM MATES SAY

I've learned to be prepared – always keep a pound on hand or in your car for the trolley (you don't want to be faffing around trying to get change when you've got a baby), always have a muslin or something on hand to wipe down wet trolleys if it's raining, and always do a wee before you leave the house because trying to do one with a baby and your shopping is not fun! And the big one is to remember that all babies cry, and if yours does it when you're at the check-out, it's only because everybody hates queuing!

Izzy, mum of two

The hardest bit is actually when you get home and need to get your baby and your shopping into the house, especially if you can't park right outside. I find it's best to put the baby just inside first in the car seat and then quickly get everything in. Better than a car full of melting fish fingers!

Jo, mum of one

Just do online shopping. Duh. One of my daughter's first words was 'Ocado' ...

Nicky, mum of two

Conversations from inside the baby bubble

We mean well, we really do, but there's something about becoming a mum that makes us lose all sense of perspective ...

Friend: 'Do you know who you're going to vote for in the election?'

You: 'Which election?'

Friend: 'The one happening tomorrow.'

You: <blank face>

You: 'I think he seems like he's going to be really musical, what do you think?'

Partner: 'I don't know, babe, he's five weeks old.'

You: 'I just think he seems to have a good sense of rhythm, look at how he's wriggling his leg in time with the music on the telly.'

Partner: 'I think he's just doing a poo.'

Your mum: 'So, I'm arranging your dad's birthday
      lunch. It's at 2.00 pm at Quite Nice Family-Friendly
      Restaurant.'
You: 'Two pm! That's not going to work for us. That's
      when she has her sleep. Come on, you can't possibly
      expect us to make it at that time. Also, imagine the
      traffic when we drive home! She hates traffic lights.
      Wouldn't it be a lot better for everyone if we did an
      11.00 am brunch?'

You on mum forum: 'Can anyone recommend any
      reputable baby modelling agencies?'
The world: 'Oh, she thinks her baby is cuter than all the
      other babies. Bless . . . '

You: 'I just can't believe she brought him to baby group
      when he had a runny nose! It's so irresponsible.'
Mum friend: 'Yeah, I know, they're all going to get colds
      now. And she didn't even mention it in advance! So
      rude. Do you think we should say something?'

You: 'Yep, it's all going brilliantly, thanks. But check out
      this poonami! So gross!'
Your WhatsApp group of work colleagues: *block number*

You: 'You should know never to ring our doorbell
      between 9.00 and 10.00am! My baby was napping
      and now she's woken up. Do you have any idea how
      stressful this is?'
Postman: 'Can you just sign for this please.'

WHAT OUR MUM MATES SAY

I cringe when I look back at some of the stuff I talked about in the early days, especially with my first. But we all do it – obsessing about your baby and having no regard for anything or anyone else is a sign that you're a good mum, right?

Mary, mum of two

I had a premature baby and me and my gang of preemies could – and did – chat for hours about how old our baby 'really' was. Doing the maths of 'corrected ages' when you are sleep deprived involves some pretty complex calculations and amused us for hours. Even now I realise that is seriously boring chat for anyone not in the bubble!

Kirsty, mum of one

One of the first big surprises when I became pregnant was how long my other mum friends and I could chat about buggies. Who knew there was so much to say about travel systems and cup holders. Reckon I could write a pretty decent dissertation on the pros and cons of brand X versus brand Y.

Ruby, mum of one

I made a special 'the baby is sleeping' sign to stick on the front door to stop people from knocking. It didn't seem to work.

Jo, mum of one

———————————————

4

Six to twelve weeks

When you start to find your mum stride

You're a car seat pro. You could change a nappy in your sleep (in fact, you regularly do). You've even found a way to wash your hair occasionally. Sure, you're knackered, but the shellshock of the first few weeks is wearing off and your baby is starting to smile back at you, which makes everything worth it.

There might even be a routine of sorts forming; we don't mean of the seven to seven sleeping variety – that is still a pipe dream for now – but you've got to know your baby and, generally, unless they're in the middle of a growth spurt/developmental leap/random disruptive whim, there are likely to be a few things that have become predictable. They might start napping at regular intervals, for instance, rather than dozing off in your arms willy-nilly, and their feeding will soon settle into something of a pattern too if it hasn't already.

All of which means you can start actually doing stuff,

hurrah! In addition, all those pesky visitors have gone back to their normal lives, leaving you and your baby to your own devices. So, what happens next?

How to get two hours to yourself – and what to do with them

The first time you leave your baby with someone else can be extremely nerve-racking. It's not just that you've spent the last few weeks attached to this little human – they spent nine months lounging inside your body too, so it's natural that you'll feel weird to not have them within arm's length. But the day will come when your partner or your mum or some kindly friend will say 'Why don't you have some time to yourself?' and at first you'll say no, but then realise that the baby is fed, reasonably content and there's really no reason at all why you can't do your own thing for an hour or two. And that concept is more exhilarating than you ever thought possible. But, what are you actually going to do?

1. Wave your arms around a lot

Even if you just go for a stroll to the nearest shop, you'll be doing it unencumbered by your buggy or sling, your changing bag and your somewhat demanding baby. It's just you, your arms, and the absolute minimum amount of possessions you can get away with. To start with, your arms will feel really weird, all unnecessarily long and loose, but then you'll get used to it and it feels so good. This is really living, right?

2. Get pampered

You could get your hair trimmed, your nails done, your eyebrows preened or your, er, bits tended to (if you're sufficiently recovered from the birth to let anyone near that particular zone). Opportunities to make yourself feel pretty are few and far between in the early days, but most beauty treatments are pretty quick, and if you find somewhere close to home, you won't have to worry about not making it home in time for any kind of baby-related emergency (including your boobs exploding).

3. Do the shopping

This doesn't sound like a treat, but it's amazing how a quick solo trip to the supermarket can feel like a night out if you haven't got to drag a squawking baby there with you. You can spend as long as you like deliberating over broccoli sub-categories and even have a cuppa in the cafe afterwards. The only problem? Sometimes supermarkets are *full* of kids, so your supposed baby-free time might feel a little compromised.

4. Read something

If books that aren't about babies still feel a bit challenging, a magazine will do. Put your phone and its bizarre Google history away and unwind with some old-school printed entertainment. It feels oddly decadent. And gives you something else to talk about – imagine!

5. Sleep

Well, duh. Two hours to frolic outside sounds nice in theory, but what you really want to do is shut your eyes. And that's just fine. Sleeping when you're not responsible for a tiny human is way more satisfying and relaxing than trying to get some kip when you just know you'll be woken up by a needy small person within minutes. Get your lovely partner/mum/pal to take the baby out and sink into that bed. Sweet dreams.

WHAT OUR MUM MATES SAY

My baby was about eight weeks old when I first left him, to go to my friend's hen do. I only went to the afternoon tea part, and made my husband wait in the park over the road, because I knew my baby wouldn't go more than two hours without being breastfed. It felt bizarre to be putting make-up on and strolling into a fancy hotel, but I'm so glad I did, even though I had to ignore what felt like an actual magnetic pull back to my baby!

Liz, mum of two

I went to my local shop for milk (for tea, of course!). I discovered when I got home that I had forgotten to pull my top back up over my bra and the nursing clasp was still undone. I was so tired I wasn't even embarrassed, just pleased I could drink more tea.

Christine, mum of two

I booked a haircut when my little boy was just a few weeks old; my mum pushed him round until I was done. I met them afterwards and he needed a feed. It was about 5 p.m. and cafes were closing so we ended up in Wetherspoon's, where there was a nice discreet booth – I was still a bit nervous about breastfeeding in public. A drunk pensioner insisted on bouncing him around once I'd finished and the moment she held him I could see the poonami erupt. I whisked him to the change room and could not believe the extent of it, it went all the way up and into his hair! I stripped him down and as I was searching for baby wipes the fire alarm went off. I had this dilemma of do I carry a naked newborn covered in poo out or pray it wasn't for real and carry on regardless? Thankfully it went off after not too long. Reckon it was the drunk pensioner who set it off. But I did think that if I'd had to carry him out, at least my hair looked good.

Ruth, mum of one

Five firsts that will melt your heart

Sure, the early days can be tiring and relentless, but we mustn't forget about the one thing that makes it all worth it – basically how freaking awesome your baby is. When you're bogged down in feeds and nappy changes, look out for the little moments you'll cherish for ever. Cheesy? Sure. But having a baby seems to bring out the cheese in us ...

1. The first time they smile or laugh

Newborn babies are cute, but a little bit blank – it can be a while before you feel like you're getting very much back from them. The first time they smile, you might dismiss it as wind, but soon you realise they're smiling because you're smiling, or laughing because you're making funny faces, and it is the best feeling in the whole actual wide world. Good luck trying to get it on camera, though. They're changeable little buggers.

2. The first time someone you love holds them

Whether it's your partner, your mum or one of your dearest friends, seeing your brilliant baby in the arms of someone you love can be a big old gooey moment. In fact, you'll be so utterly consumed with taking in the beautiful sight that you might even forget that this is your big chance to go and do a wee/have a shower/eat your lunch two-handed.

3. The first time a stranger says something nice

We dismiss strangers when they make unhelpful comments, but when they say something nice – perhaps how beautiful your baby is, or how well-behaved they are, or just what a lovely cardigan they're wearing – it's a whole different story and can make our whole day. If you're feeling low and need a little boost, hang around where there are lots of clucky old ladies and this might even become a regular occurrence.

4. The first time you're called mum

We don't mean when the baby itself calls you mum – that's many, many months away – but the first time you're referred to in public as their mum, usually by some kind of health official. It's a strange identity shift and might even freak you out a bit, but it will make you feel all tingly too – likewise, the first time you refer to them as your child. Using the words 'my son' or 'my daughter' still feels awfully grown up though – we find 'my little boy' far easier to say while just about keeping a straight face.

5. The first time you feel like you've done a good job

Whether it's a seamless nappy change or a shopping trip that went without incident, those little 'I've got this!' moments early on, no matter how fleeting or infrequent they are, are worth holding on to. When your pre-baby life involved giving dead-important presentations or defending criminals or transplanting kidneys, you'll feel silly to be giving yourself a pat on the back for performing such mundane tasks, but it's really important to acknowledge that you're doing a decent job of this whole mum thing.

WHAT OUR MUM MATES SAY

Early on I got a phone call from the health centre asking to speak to 'Rosie's mum'. I said 'Sure, I'll get her ...' before realising they, of course, meant me. I felt very silly, but it was a big change from being known by my actual name!

Sarah, mum of two

Some of my best mum moments in the early days came when I was feeding my baby. I struggled with it at first, so I'll never forget the first time he paused mid-feed to look up at me and gave me a big soppy smile. It just makes it all worth it.

Izzy, mum of two

The six types of mum friend you need in your life

When you have a baby, your identity gets a huge shake-up. Your daily routine is unrecognisable, you dress differently and you have opinions about things you didn't know it was possible to have opinions about, like pram brands and places it's OK to change a nappy (on the ground at the park: yes; in the living room: depends who's watching – and inhaling).

If your existing friends don't have babies yet, or have kids of a different age, you'll suddenly feel like an alien, and you'll desperately need fellow aliens for late-night WhatsApp chats and early morning, swingside cake scoffing. There are all sorts of ways to make mum friends – antenatal classes, baby groups and, of course, this awesome app called Mush – but one thing's for sure, you can never have enough of them. Especially because they will all fulfil different roles in your shiny new mum world.

Of course, the big question is, which one of these new mum clichés are you? Or are you, in fact, a little bit of all of them?

1. Knit-your-own-nappy mum

How to spot her It's hard to get a good look at her because there's a baby covering her entire body and face. Yep, no buggies here, she's a baby-wearer and proud – and definitely not in a Baby Björn, perish the thought. She's passionate about breastfeeding, she uses cloth nappies (or at least eco-friendly ones) and in her house CBeebies is a swear word.

Why you need her She's full of cool ideas that you might never have thought of. The main one being: if in doubt, put coconut oil on it. Organic, obvs.

2. Sign-foetus-up-for-the-2032-London-Marathon mum

How to spot her When you stumble into your relaxed, weekly nursery rhymes session, she's already there, right at the front, bellowing out 'The Grand Old Duke Of York' in three languages. She's obsessed with her birth story: 'Out in three pushes, just a paracetamol'. If little Beatrice isn't walking by nine months, she'll wonder where she went wrong.

Why you need her She'll take you to all the best baby classes – she has spreadsheets for this stuff. Plus, she makes you feel dead chilled in comparison.

3. Take-baby-to-A&E-because-its-fart-smelled-off mum

How to spot her She's the one cleaning baby Leo's precious bum with cooled boiled water well into his second year. She gets through four bottles of hand sanitiser a week. She's on first-name terms with the entire staff of the local A&E and she sends you panicky messages at 3.00 am, asking if it's normal for babies to smile in their sleep or if it's a sign of a rare neurological disorder.

Why you need her She's there for you when you're feeling anxious too. Baby got a snotty nose? She'll be straight round with her bag of magic potions. Just nobody breathe.

4. Back-in-the-size-eight-skinnies mum

How to spot her She's clutching a glass of Prosecco and wearing hot pants. But you're at baby massage class and it's 10.20 am. Sure, she loves little Amelie with all her heart, but getting her life back is a big priority. Sleep training commences at three days old, and baby spends every Friday night at Granny's house before the first month is out.

Why you need her Because when your baby is six months old and you still haven't been apart for more than two hours, she'll drag you to the pub to bitch about ex-boyfriends, and you'll feel more like your old self too.

5. Still-functioning-thanks-only-to-caffeine-and-cuddles mum

How to spot her She's crying, she's filthy and she's shakily clutching a giant latte. She just fell asleep standing up in front of the swings. Smiley little Reuben is a joy during the day, but has never slept more than twenty minutes at a time at night. Her husband no longer speaks. A glutton for punishment, she'll somehow be pregnant again within the year. 'I've never been happier,' she sobs.

Why you need her Because we all have days when we're her. And when we're having a good run, it makes us kinder to those who aren't. Plus, she's always available for coffee. Really strong coffee.

6. The dad friend

How to spot her Well, her is a him, that's the main giveaway. Despite the existence of shared parental leave and the fact that it's the twenty-first century, there still aren't many men on the maternity circuit, particularly at the little baby stage. So dads can look a bit awkward, desperate to get out and about and fill their days, but too worried about accidentally wading into some banter about vaginal stitches to strike up a conversation with all those flipping mums.

Why you need him To talk about something other than vaginal stitches, tbh. Dad friends can generally offer a different perspective on parenting. Also, he might well be feeling lonelier than you can imagine. Let him in!

WHAT OUR MUM MATES SAY

Before the baby actually comes you might think 'But I've got loads of mates!', but then you realise it's not enough – you need friends with babies exactly the same age who live really, really close. In the early days, even six weeks is a huge age gap and it will feel like they're going through totally different things. I wish I'd known this before, as I would've made a lot more effort earlier!

Becca, mum of two

To start with you might just talk (obsessively!) about babies with your mum mates, but with the good ones it soon goes beyond that. It's like starting school or uni or a new job – there are people you just talk to because you have basic things in common, but after a few months you know which ones are going to stick.

Luisa, mum of one

I felt really lonely in the first few weeks because I didn't know anyone nearby with a baby. All my friends were at work and I hadn't done antenatal classes because I was busy moving house. I had to really force myself to get out and talk to people. I didn't used to be shy but having a baby can make you feel so vulnerable! Sometimes it feels like people are in cliques already but it's not really the case. I made myself talk to people even when I didn't really feel like it, but it always made a difference to my day.

Jo, mum of one

Sensory? Massage? Baby bounce? WTF are these classes and when should you go?

When you finally feel ready to leave the house on a regular basis, the options can be overwhelming. And if you're a doer of a person, you can end up throwing yourself at activities before your baby is remotely interested. Here's what to bother with, and when.

Newborn to six weeks: baby massage

You want to do a class already? Sheesh, you're good at this. But the thing is, your newborn is basically a cute accessory at this point. If you're a total joiner, baby massage is a good option for the early days. It's pretty gentle, can help with some of those early wind issues (the baby's, not yours – that's a whole different subject), and if you've got a group of mum friends already, you can get an instructor to come to your house for a private class, which is infinitely more fun with added cake and Prosecco.

Four to twelve weeks: the pub

Why bother paying to sing 'Incy Wincy Spider' when you can just go out for long lunches and pelvic floor banter? At this point, your baby is small and portable enough to drag anywhere, and cute enough that nobody will mind if he or she kicks off. Enjoy your freedom – when they're bigger, you'll be so obsessed with naps that it will feel impossible to coordinate schedules with your mum chums, and your little darling will want to throw food everywhere.

Newborn to six months: parent and baby cinema

Baby cinema is genius – you get to feel culturally savvy while your baby does what it does at home anyway: feed, sleep and squawk, without judgement. Make the most of it in the early months – soon they'll be too big, flaily and shouty to sit through a two-hour thought-provoking drama.

Four to eight months: baby sensory

Baby sensory is just a fancy name for a room full of women (and the occasional, apologetic-looking man) flapping scarves around and wondering if bubble solution will stain their suede boots. But middle-aged babies love it – especially as the group leaders are usually utterly transfixing, failed kids' TV presenters with booming voices and fabulously garish hair.

Six to twelve months: anything noisy

Hate nursery rhymes? Sorry, but you should've stayed on the pill: you're going to be hearing a lot of them. Soon you'll even have a favourite – you'll say it's your baby's favourite, but everyone knows you just love 'Horsey Horsey'. Baby Bounce classes (free at libraries across the land) are a good place to start, but wherever you live, you'll find a church hall or pub function room with a variation on the same theme. Your baby will love getting to jangle the selection of musical instruments. You'll love having fellow tired humans to chat to.

Twelve months plus: the park

Your baby is now essentially a puppy and must be exercised accordingly. Grab a coat and a coffee and off you trot.

WHAT OUR MUM MATES SAY

If your baby is anything other than very sleepy and compliant, avoid baby yoga classes like the plague. They were a humiliating disaster for me – the yoga teacher said, 'What's wrong with your baby? She sounds colicky, it's probably because you had such a difficult unnatural birth.' Officially the least Zen thing ever. But I felt like I needed to go to prove something so I went back several times. Second time around I didn't do anything that didn't make me and my second baby – another diva! – happy and calm. I spent a lot of time cuddling her in a dark room to keep her asleep while I read books on my phone.

Nicky, mum of two

I think baby classes in the early weeks and months are really just a good opportunity to get out of the house and meet other mums. I started baby massage with my son when he was twelve days old and although he just fed and screamed if I even attempted to strip him down for a massage, it was great to be out, chat to people and eat cake.

Eimear, mum of two

I loved mum and baby yoga. The class I went to was in a lovely space and we'd have tea, biscuits and lovely chats there after. I think it's really important to do something for yourself in the early days if you can – I also joined a mum choir!

Olivia, mum of one

I made the most of the local library and drop-in sessions, because I found it tricky to commit to things where you have to book and pay ahead. It would invariably coincide with the baby deciding to nap.

Kate, mum of one

Baby cinema was the best. I went every week from about six weeks to six months, and it was oddly relaxing, despite all the wriggly, screamy babies. I just zoned out with a packet of Minstrels, and got my boob out if my baby stirred! Bliss. And despite the fact that I had no clue what was going on in the news, I've never been so knowledgeable about films. I basically only had another baby so I could go again, and made sure our toddler was at nursery on the cinema days!

Michelle, mum of two

My baby sensory class was wonderful. Somehow walking round with rubber gloves on your feet pretending to be a duck at 9 am just made sense.

Freda, mum of two

I remember on one of my early trips to baby cinema with my new mum friends, I thought I had it nailed: happy, sleeping baby in a carrier, buggy and other paraphernalia at home. But then I realised she was sleeping in a puddle of poo – aargh! I scooped her up and headed to the disabled loo, sweating. I peeled everything off her – she was completely saturated – and slopped it all into the bin. Clean nappy on. All going great(ish). That's when I realised when skipping out of the house, feeling completely liberated,

I'd failed to pack any change of clothes. Do I ask my new friends for help? Will they shun me for being a shit (pardon the pun) mum? Do I just leave? I totally wanted to do the latter but my stuff was still in there. And I loved my sunglasses. I fronted it out – laughed it off (while dying inside) and bundled her up in an oversized muslin. I will never forget the fear of being judged by those other new mums. I felt such a failure. But really – none of them cared at all. I now know that what seems huge at the time will soon be forgotten. By others, even if not by you. But at least you have a story to tell!

Jo, mum of one

Getting to know your new mum wardrobe

No matter how fashionable you used to be – maybe you even worked in fashion (mwah!) – things will change a bit when you become a mum. All of your previous good taste will be transferred to your baby, who looks cool and stylish and so on-trend at all times, while your own wardrobe will have an emphasis on practical and comfortable. Here are a few staple items that you'll hate yourself for wearing on a daily basis ...

Stripy tops

What is it with mums and stripy tops? Who decided this was our uniform? What if we don't even like stripes? There are so many new mums rocking Breton stripes that if an alien visited the planet, he or she would be forgiven for thinking these were issued postnatally, along with the red book and all those fricking pamphlets. The truth is, it starts in pregnancy (*so* many maternity clothes are striped; because of course we really want to look even wider) and is a hard habit to break.

So many leggings

Nobody likes leggings. But everyone's got some. And they're so easy to wear. So you might find yourself wearing them every day, in a variety of shades of black. High-waisted ones are particularly gentle on C-section scars, and, regardless of how you gave birth, there's absolutely no way you'll be wanting to wear jeans any time soon.

Trousers that look a bit like pyjamas

God bless fashion for bringing back patterned trousers a few years back. It means that our pyjamas are interchangeable

with our actual clothes, and that's an ideal state of affairs for a new mum, even if we now look like our actual mum in our natty floral slacks.

Jazzy trainers

You used to love a statement shoe. But it's no longer practical to wear heels every day – or indeed, ever – so instead you've developed a penchant for snazzy trainers. Sparkly Converse, fluorescent high tops, leopard-print plimsolls ... you've got the lot. It's your way of showing your individuality, in case the stripy top and leggings suggested otherwise. Oh wait, the woman next to you at baby sensory has got the same ones. Bugger. Better buy some more.

A practical coat with loads of pockets

Screw chic, tailored jackets. You need a waterproof, hooded anorak type affair which has ample pockets to house your phone, a packet of raisins, a sippy cup and Sophie la Girafe.

Layers and layers and layers

If you're breastfeeding, your top half will be forever wrapped in layers that you can pull up, down, in, out and shake all about – whatever provides adequate access for your baby while not giving you frozen nips when you inevitably have to whip them out on a park bench. Some of these layers are probably stripy. All of them are stretchy.

Food

Yes, you wear food now. Your own, because you ate it too fast. Your baby's regurgitated milk. Further down the line, sweet potato that they've hurled at you. Wearing patterns helps. So does perfume, if you remember what that is.

WHAT OUR MUM MATES SAY

I often look longingly into my wardrobe at all the gorgeous dresses I used to wear every day. One day in the future we'll be reunited ... but sadly I might need to lose the baby weight first.

Izzy, mum of two

I found myself googling 'best black leggings' recently and then had to take a long hard look at myself. I'm not sure what I expect a pair of leggings to be able to do that the eight pairs I own already aren't already doing.

Jo, mum of one

How to like your partner again, and maybe even give them a cuddle

After having a baby one of the biggest transformations isn't your once-immaculate living room, or your once-even-more-immaculate pelvic floor, but your relationship. The baby might have come into the world because of the love between you, but that doesn't mean it's all flowers and rainbows after they're actually born. There are lots of different issues that can crop up in the early months. Here are a few of the most common, and how to tackle them.

The issue: bonding with the baby – or lack of

If you're breastfeeding, your partner might feel like they don't get opportunities to bond with the baby. Funnily enough, getting to change nappies instead does feel a bit like a, well, booby prize. If you don't want to implement the odd bottle (or your pesky baby simply won't take one), there are still things your partner can do to feel more physically bonded with the fruit of their loins. Bathing with them is one lovely one – babies are generally in a good mood at bath time – and bringing the baby into bed in the morning for giggly cuddles is another. Your partner can also read to them from the word go. Sure, the baby doesn't have a clue what's going on, but you'll fall in love with your beloved all over again when you hear them putting their heart and soul into *The Very Hungry Caterpillar.*

The issue: your envying their freedom

If you're in a trad set-up, where you're on maternity leave while they bound off to work every day, you might find yourself resenting them getting to leave the house unencumbered by baby paraphernalia, then swanning onto public transport without a care in the world (and without being shouted at to fold up the damned pram when *the baby is sleeping*), guzzling hot drinks at their desk, idly tucking into a burrito for lunch and maybe even having a cheeky drink after work. You watch the clock all afternoon, desperate for them to get home so you can do a wee by yourself, and they don't understand what the fuss is about. Encouraging them to take the odd day or half-day off just to hang out with the baby will help or this might be a good opportunity to look into shared parental leave. It's the only way they'll truly understand the ups and downs of spending every waking (and sleeping) hour with a baby.

The issue: competitive tiredness

You're knackered because you're surgically attached to a baby 24/7. They're knackered because they're getting up and going to work, but no longer getting very much downtime outside of this – as well as getting woken regularly in the night, even if they've been shipped off to the spare room for the time being. It can be a seriously tough time, and a huge source of tension early on. It's important to acknowledge that you are both entitled to be tired, and that there is no way of scientifically measuring this, so stop acting like you're competing in the fatigue Olympics. Instead, take it in turns to have little lie-ins (like, 8.00 am) at weekends and try to give each other mini windows of downtime at other times – even if it's just fifteen minutes when they get in from work, when you get to go upstairs and have a shower by yourself.

The issue: cold hard cash

If you're on mat leave – particularly if you're on statutory mater-nity pay, aka not much more than pocket money – chances are you're probably feeling pretty skint. And yet still you buy stuff – the odd coffee and cake out, a few quid on groups and classes, irresistibly cute baby clothes, 3.00 am Amazon purchases that will almost certainly revolutionise the entire household's sleep – and that might well wind your partner up if they're con-tributing a bigger chunk of cash to the household funds. The solution? Explain that you *need* to leave the house and do stuff for your sanity, so there needs to be a budget for that, but try to curb the spending – or at least sell off all the tat you haven't used before you buy all of the new things.

The issue: the state of the house

Babies are tiny, and yet one moves in and suddenly it looks as though you live in a war zone. What's that about? Even if you and/or your partner used to be Monica Geller levels of par-ticular, you'll both struggle to keep up to your high standards once your home's been invaded by Hurricane Newborn – and, as we all know, there's nothing like a row about dirty socks on the floor. A professional cleaner is a huge luxury, but throw your money at one if you can afford it – it's cheaper than marriage counselling. If that's not an option, getting a bit more structured with your cleaning routine can help. Adjust your expectations a little bit, and choose one or two jobs that you can realistically get done between you at the weekend. Alternatively, just live in squalor like the rest of us. Or wait until your little one is crawling and then attach sponges to their hands and feet. Kidding. Ish.

The issue: lack of touchyfeelyness

It's not just the fact that the baby spends most of its time lounging around your body, like a human electric fence that wards off all invasions from other sources, but the fact that even when they're tucked up in their bed, sometimes you feel totally touched-out and the last thing you want to do is get snuggly with another person. Plus, you might well still be feeling vulnerable about your body post-birth – whether it's worries about your weight or fear of pain if you get jiggy. Nobody expects to be at it like rabbits in the early months, but your partner might not understand exactly how you're feeling – and if they're keeping their distance as well then you might start feeling paranoid too. Obviously, be honest with them about how you're feeling – but if you can find the energy to put your head on their shoulder for a few seconds before zonking out, it might help reconnect you.

The issue: no quality time

OK, so deep down you suspected life with a baby wouldn't involve leisurely afternoons in the pub reading the papers and romantic getaways in seaside towns, but when your relationship suddenly feels just so tediously functional, revolving around nappy changes and feeds and, later, nursery drop-offs and nit remedies, it can be hard to handle. If you're not ready to leave your baby with anyone else, it doesn't mean you can't carve out a bit of quality time. Even just enjoying the same box set instead of spending the evening staring at separate devices will help bond you. Eat something nice *et voilà*: you've just had a date night.

WHAT OUR MUM MATES SAY

Some brilliant friends of ours knew we desperately needed some time together but that we weren't confident enough to think we could do it, so they forced themselves into our house when our little girl was a couple of months old, and made us go out for dinner locally. We were only gone for an hour or so but it felt like a dirty weekend. Don't turn down opportunities to spend time together, it can make a massive difference, even if all you talk about is your baby!

Saskia, mum of one

Housework was a big source of stress early on for us. My partner couldn't understand why I wasn't keeping on top of things because he didn't know what it was really like to look after a baby all day. We couldn't afford a cleaner while I was on maternity leave so we just had to get more organised, plus my parents paid for a deep clean for us for Christmas, which we really appreciated. Now I'm back at work we do have a cleaner and it's a much happier household!

Becca, mum of two

How to keep on top of baby admin

Oh man, nobody said that being a mum would be like being an executive assistant to the world's most demanding and irrational boss. As well as the small matter of keeping your baby fed, clothed, rested and entertained, there's a whole heap of admin attached to motherhood which will keep your diary full over the early months. Here are a few of the 'highlights' ...

The six- to eight-week check

This happens with your GP and is for you *and* the baby – to check how you're healing up (physically and emotionally) post-birth and to weigh and measure your baby. It's also a chance for you to bring up any concerns about their health and to discuss all the stuff you've been WhatsApping your mum mates about late at night.

Health visitor appointments

Although the schedule can vary regionally, most families will have a couple of home visits in the very early months, followed by checks at around nine months and then two years. A good health visitor can be a lifeline, there to help you with anything you might be struggling with.

Weighing clinics

Some new mums go to the weighing clinics religiously – and not just to keep track of their baby, but also to get out of the house and chat to other mums. You'll usually leave with an anecdote about your baby peeing all over the scales, plus it's a great place to get reassurance about feeding, weaning and your baby's general development. Second-time mums are conspicuous by their absence.

Vaccinations

Your baby's vaccination schedule will be in your red book (officially your new mum bible – well, after this one), but generally they start kicking in from about eight weeks, feel awfully regular for a while, and then tail off. None of them are compulsory, but your GP and health visitor will strongly advise you to take up everything offered. Yes, your baby will probably be deeply unimpressed by being poked with needles, but it's all over very quickly, and we guarantee you're more traumatised than they are.

Money, money, money

Most families are entitled to basic child benefit (what we called 'family allowance' in ye olden days), but make sure you do your research to find out what else you might be able to claim – plus bear in mind that if one of you is a high earner there can be tax and repayment implications.

Childcare

You might have just gone on mat leave, but if you're planning to send your baby to nursery at some point in the next year, you might want to start doing your research now (see the dedicated childcare guide in the final section of the book – or just bury your head in the sand and freak out in a few months). Waaah!

WHAT OUR MUM MATES SAY

I found my mum friends invaluable for muddling through with all the baby admin and making sure I didn't miss anything. It's good to have one with a baby a few weeks older, who has to suss it all out first!

Izzy, mum of two

It's all about the red book. I made the rookie error of forgetting to take the red book with me to my baby's first vaccinations, and the nurse looked at me wryly and said, 'First baby?' That thing is your bible. Albeit a bible with loads of random pieces of paper falling out of it, and probably covered in tea stains by now too ...

Jo, mum of one

But what if you're doing it a different way?

We know that not all mums are parenting the 'conventional' way, and that becoming a mum is hard enough without any extra factors thrown in. We're proud that on Mush we have every kind of mum under the sun using the app to make their mum life as fun, sociable and supportive as possible. So, what kind of hurdles might be thrown your way if you happen to tick any of the following boxes?

Single mums

Whether your relationship broke down while you were pregnant, there was never a proper relationship in the first place or you've actively chosen to go it alone via a donor, embarking on motherhood alone can be very daunting indeed. From picking a birth partner to the logistics of the early days post-birth when you don't have anyone around to do the heavy lifting to the constant extra strain on finances, everything is that bit tougher when you're on your own. But you're *not* on your own – there are loads and loads of mums in the same boat, and teaming up with them can make all the difference – especially at weekends, when it feels like everyone else is playing happy families. Plus, let's look at the pros: all the decisions to be made about your baby are yours and yours alone, and you can be all the more proud of every little thing they do.

Mums of kids with additional needs

Perhaps you knew your baby was different during the pregnancy, perhaps there were problems during the birth or perhaps issues have made themselves evident over time; whatever the case, you're going to need a lot more support than your average mum – emotionally, practically and perhaps financially. Some couples find that parenting a child with additional needs can put a strain on their relationship, while others develop an 'us vs the world' approach that makes them stronger than ever. Either way, get all the support you can from friends, family, health professionals and charities. You'll be surprised how many people in your extended network have insight and experience of the very things you're going through. Your baby's milestones might be different from the norm, but their journey is all the more special for it.

Same-sex couples

Good news: it's the twenty-first century, which means lots and lots of same-sex couples are embarking on parenthood. The only big difference between you and other couples is the fact that there are fewer of you around, and while the mum friends you do make are just lovely, you may find yourself craving the company of other same-sex couples. Depending on where you live, seeking them out can be challenging, but ask around on social media (and make sure you've chosen the relevant tags on your Mush profile) and you'll soon find groups to join.

Mums of multiples

So, it turns out not everyone gives birth to just one baby. If you're a mum of twins, triplets or – eek – more (and you have time to read a book? Blimey), you really have your work cut out. You might feel like mums of singletons don't understand what you're going through and if they say how knackered they are, you'll want to smother them with Ewan the Dream Sheep, but grinning and bearing it, while looking for other mums of multiples to hang out with, is a far better option.

Mums from overseas

If you're not from round here, there are all sorts of reasons why becoming a mum can be that bit more isolating. There could be language or cultural barriers, or perhaps you just really miss your family and feel envious of the mums you meet who have supportive relatives just round the corner. Again, a quick search on social media, or indeed Mush, will find mums who – literally – speak the same language. Remember, too, how lucky your baby is to be brought up with different cultural influences and potentially more than one language.

WHAT OUR MUM MATES SAY

Bringing up our daughter in a different country – we're Portuguese but now live in London – hasn't always been easy; it's tough when your family are thousands of miles away, and when we do get to see them, it's expensive, and intense! I compensated for this by trying really hard to make lots of mum friends in my area. Some of them are from overseas too, so they totally get it, but it doesn't really matter – it's more about just building a big support network.

Maria, mum of one

Being a single parent is tough but it means I have a brilliant bond with my daughter which I hope never fades. And there are advantages too – when she's with her dad, I always make loads of plans, so I have a better social life than most of my married friends!

Rachel, mum of one

5

Three to six months

When you didn't realise you'd still be this tired

Goodbye, newborn phase. The 'fourth trimester' is over and your baby is now officially an actual baby, not a weird, wriggly, alien newborn thing. Exciting times. And there's a lot to look forward to: so many developmental milestones are looming, you get loads more interaction from them, plus – best of all – they're in a whole new clothes size. This is an excuse for buying even more cute things (or receiving even more, if you've been savvy/lucky enough to sync this stage with Christmas).

Of course, there are tough bits too (four-month sleep regression, we mean you) but we hope that by now you're building a good support network and enjoying more days than you're dreading. Once again, with some help from our trusty mum mates, here's a little preview of the next few months.

The ups and downs of your baby no longer being a newborn

Some people absolutely adore the newborn stage; they're also the kind of people who love YouTube videos of kittens. OK, rubbish analogy – everyone loves YouTube videos of kittens. The newborn human bit, though, is more divisive, and it's totally normal if deep down you can't wait for it to be over. If this is you, your time has now come ...

They might be sleeping through the night

The good news is, most babies aged three months are capable of sleeping through the night. The bad news is, that doesn't mean they're going to. Because, while some babies *can* comfortably go without a feed for most of the night from this sort of age, most of them still wake for night feeds or just extra cuddles, because they enjoy the closeness and general disruption that it brings. It's normal. Babies have been expertly manufactured for thousands of years to wake regularly – it protects them from SIDS, among other things.

Even if you do have a good sleeper on your lucky, lucky hands, you should know that the dreaded four-month sleep regression is looming and that's one milestone that has wiped the smug smile off many a mum's face who thought they had this sleeping thing down (we speak from experience ...). But don't panic! By now you'll be used to the ups and downs of baby sleep (or lack thereof) and can muddle through with your mum friends – and lots and lots of caffeine.

They can do stuff

We're not saying you can send them out to work just yet, but your baby is now way more alert and animated than they were before. Over the next few months, they'll master all sorts of dead-useful skills. You can prop them up in stuff, play with them more and enjoy their GSOH – they might enjoy a game of peekaboo, for instance. If they're super-advanced, they might even master crawling at around six months, but most babies are still largely immobile at this age, which means you can still plonk them in a bouncer or similar while you go about your business.

They know who they are

Your baby will soon start responding to their own name, so we hope you picked a good one. The downside to this sense of identity is that they might start to become more wary of strangers. Whereas most newborns can be passed around willy-nilly (unless they're peckish), as they grow up babies become a bit more clingy, and stranger danger can start to creep in. On the plus side, it's always handy when you need to get away from someone you don't like at a party.

You can plan your days more

You've probably spent the last few months going with the flow, with your baby dropping off whenever they damned-well pleased and wreaking havoc with any plans you foolishly made. Now, you can potentially regain a bit of control. At three months, most babies are on three clear naps that you can plan your day around, and before long this will cut down to two.

The two-nap thing is *great* for days out or visiting friends and family, because they can have sleeps in the car or buggy for both legs of the journey, while you can all enjoy the time in between. It also means you can start committing to regular baby classes if that's your bag, although the mischievous little monkeys will still do their best to throw your plans awry and fall asleep in the buggy just as you pull up to the venue. Many a fiver has been wasted on a sleeping baby but, hey, at least it gets you out of the house, right?

They are cuter than ever

This one's actually a trick, because you will think your baby gets cuter and cuter all the time, until they become a teenager and look a bit gross. But, post-newborn phase, your baby is 'on fleek' – any crusty skin and cradle cap will start clearing up, their hair is potentially growing fast and they simply love smiling. They also look absolutely magnificent in any seasonal costumes of the era, so if it's Halloween, Easter or Christmas when you're in this phase, make the most of the photo opportunities. You won't regret it.

WHAT OUR MUM MATES SAY

I know some people love the newborn phase, but I was so relieved to get beyond it. Newborns are lovely for cuddles, but you don't get much back and they are so helpless. The next bit was fun because I could enjoy the increased inter-action, without having to worry that they would wreck the house if my back was turned!

Nicky, mum of two

The four-month sleep regression is a total bitch. I naively thought it wouldn't happen to us, as my baby was a good sleeper, but of course it did – he went from sleep-ing through to waking two or three times a night, which I know isn't *that* bad, but it was a shock to the system, especially as I had started doing a bit of work ... in theory while he slept. But it does pass, and my advice would be to just take each day – and night – as it comes, don't take on too much and catch up on sleep whenever you can! And don't despair, because all the cuteness makes up for it too ...

Izzy, mum of two

The bedtime routine: dream vs reality

If you've never had an evening like this, you're officially win-
ning. For everyone else, here's some reassurance.

Time: 5.23 pm

The dream Baby is playing happily on the floor with a
wooden Scandinavian toy while you knock up a delicious
tagine to be served up when Daddy gets home. In the background, Radio Four fills you in on the latest political events,
about which you have many intelligent opinions.

The reality Baby is smearing strawberries and Babybel into
your hair, but who cares as you haven't washed it for a week.
The Babybel is from six meals ago – you just haven't had
time to wipe the highchair. Your own dinner will be tackled
many hours from now. The only political activity you've
engaged in since 2013 was signing a Facebook petition to
save CBeebies, which is obviously on right now.

Time: 6.32 pm

The dream Daddy bounds through the door, clutching flowers. Your baby chooses this beautiful moment to take his first
steps, launching himself into Daddy's warm, muscular arms.

The reality You repeatedly refresh your live train arrivals
traffic app and then send a pass-agg text to Daddy: 'Assume
you're running a bit late, hope all ok, can you let me know

if you'll be back for bedtime asap as bubba's very tired xxx'. Meanwhile, 'bubba' is whacking HD Iggle Piggle with a fork.

Time: 6.59 pm

The dream You share a bubble bath with your giggling baby while Daddy sits beside you, playing acoustic guitar with his warm, muscular arms, giving 'The Wheels On The Bus' a stripped-back, Radio One Live Lounge sort of vibe.

The reality Daddy's still not home so you run the bath while letting baby have some 'nappy-free time' because you heard it's really good for them – or you got in a muddle and took his clothes off too early. He wees on the pile of clean laundry you've dumped on the floor. You pretend not to notice, since it's going to get dirty sooner or later anyway.

Time: 7.19 pm

The dream Cuddling baby in his warm, muscular arms, Daddy reads a story, putting on a variety of hilarious animal voices, and then gently passes him over to you. You breast-feed him until he's drowsy but awake, and then gently place him in the cot. He flashes you a dozy smile and falls asleep.

The reality Still no sign of Daddy, so you skip the story and pop baby on your boob. He nods off quickly – too quickly, he's going to be hungry again soon, you just know it – and you wait until your arm is dead before attempting a stealth transfer to the cot. Daddy chooses this moment to bound through the door, shouting, 'Hello! Dada's home! Am I too late for bedtime?' Baby jolts awake and cries. You stick him on your boob again.

Time: 8.14 pm

The dream You snuggle on the sofa in Daddy's warm, muscular arms and drink a respectable amount of really good wine while watching a Danish drama on Amazon Prime. And that tagine went down really well.

The reality You're still upstairs attempting something called 'shush-pat'. Daddy's watching the football. He does bring you some wine, though. 'Can I take over?', 'No, there's no point now', 'Shall I order takeaway?, 'If you want.'

Time: 10.07 pm

The dream You glide up to bed, checking in on baby on the way. He's fine, of course, and doesn't stir. Daddy flashes you a cheeky grin as you head towards the marital bed. Now it's time to make baby a little brother or sister. You're both ready. Those warm, muscular arms slide up your silk nightie ...

The reality Baby's finally asleep in his cot, so you sneak downstairs in tracksuit bottoms and an old hoodie and wolf down some lukewarm lemon chicken. You're on your third mouthful when the monitor roars at you. It's fine, you hadn't bothered to refasten your nursing bra anyway.

Time: 12.39 am

The dream Blissful, post-coital sleep in those warm, muscular arms.

The reality Daddy falls to the floor and cuts his sweaty, knobbly arm on some discarded Duplo as baby, who joined you in bed two hours ago, thrusts his warm, flabby limbs across the mattress and does a huge fart.

Time: 4.48 am

The dream Zzzzzzz.

The reality *Morning!*

WHAT OUR MUM MATES SAY

It took a long time before we had any kind of bedtime routine. Usually evenings were just a frenzied muddle of trying to remember to eat, squeezing a bath in and rocking the baby until she would sleep. But I'd usually fall asleep at the same time. When we finally got her into a proper bedtime routine and got our evenings back it was such a relief.

Luisa, mum of one

Through trial and error and reading a few baby books, I got the routine thing down early on. I knew it would help keep me sane – well, saner. Obviously things don't always go according to plan though!

Jo, mum of one

Five signs you should step away from the mum forums

Being a mum can be boring and lonely at times, which is why so many of us while away our 'spare' time (ha!) online, using other mums as our sounding boards for everything that happens in our lives – or, more likely, just digitally eavesdropping on other mums who are doing just that. But, while mum forums can be a great place to get support, advice or just to let off steam once in a while, they aren't always the healthiest places – here are a few signs that you should put the smartphone down ...

1. When someone's said they're 'not judging but . . . '

This generally means they are judging, hard. What is it about the internet that turns us back into bitchy schoolgirls? Mums saying stuff about other mums doing stuff differently from how they do stuff is a common theme on mum forums. Often this is stuff related to the raising of babies, particularly around hot topics like feeding, weaning and sleep training. While this is generally just a way to find like-minded people who'll validate their points of view, it can leave a seriously baaaaad taste in the mouth and end up with everyone involved feeling a little bit judged, actually.

2. When there's chat about sleep

If you've had a bad night, or a hundred bad nights on the trot, the last thing you need to hear about is how JonahsMummy101 has been enjoying uninterrupted nights of 7.00–7.00 bliss since Jonah was three weeks old. Similarly, if you are the mother of the prodigal sleeper, while it can be useful to swap stories of stuff that's worked in your house, resist the urge to brag, or karma will reward you with an unscheduled sleep regression.

3. When you want medical advice

Good old Dr Google. It's pretty useful that there is (legit) medical advice a few clicks away these days, but post-ing pictures of dodgy rashes on mum groups is not the best way to diagnose and can come off as a leeeeeeetle bit attention-seeking. Most groups and forums clamp down on this kind of thing and try to ban parents from posting medical queries, but still they rumble on – we all know that when we've got concerns about our baby there is no shutting us up. Needless to say, if you're genuinely worried about your baby – or indeed yourself – brave the queues at the walk-in centre.

4. When you just spilled your guts

If you find yourself turning to online communities whenever you have a problem, spilling the beans on issues in your relationship, your annoying sister-in-law and your financial woes, you might want to take a step back. Again, the support from strangers can make a huge difference, but ideally not to the detriment of your real-life relationships. Also, there's the privacy issue – how would you feel if you caught a friend or family member sharing all your secrets online behind a thinly-veiled username?

5. When you can't understand a bloody word anyone is saying

So, you BD'ed with your DH and now you have a gorgeous LO (your PFB) who, BTW, you EBF and BLW, but your MIL thinks you should FF so she can have more QT with your DC. Lost? Then step away from the forums and go and have a normal conversation instead. LOL.

WHAT OUR MUM MATES SAY

I got into using mum forums when I was trying to conceive (TTC!) our baby. I found them really useful to the point of obsession, but by the time our baby was actually born I got a bit fed up with it all. Now I mostly just browse them if I have a specific query rather than chatting all day – it's not as if I have time now anyway! I do keep in touch with a couple of mums I met that way, though.

Sarah, mum of one

My husband got really annoyed with me spending my evenings using mum forums and chat group. He was convinced it was making me compare our baby to other people's babies too much, but actually I was just looking for reassurance. I do still go on them, just when he's not looking!

Mary, mum of two

How to get through the day when you've had no sleep

You're not an idiot – you knew way before you ditched contraception that having a baby means both the quality and quantity of your sleep would be compromised. But somehow it still comes as quite a shock. Even if your baby is a good sleeper from the start (who is this mythical creature and where can we get one?), there will be days when you feel hit-by-a-ton-of-bricks exhausted. What to do?

1. Get out

You can barely find the energy to lift a finger of toast to your mouth, but you'll feel so much better if you get up, out and move around. Even just a quick walk around the block will take the edge off. And they say that fresh air helps babies sleep. Got to be worth a shot, right?

2. Find some mum mates

You know who else is tired? Other mums. Drag your eye bags to the nearest coffee shop, children's centre or someone's house, and compare war wounds. There will always be someone who's had a worse night than you, promise.

3. Ring your favourite person

If you have a mum, sister or mate who always cheers you up, reach out to them. You never know, they might be at a loose end and come and hang out with you during your time of need. Or at the very least they can distract you by telling you funny stories/cooing over how cute your baby is.

4. Tackle the day strategically

If you've ever had a boring job, you'll know that the best way to get through a rubbish day is to divide it up into manageable chunks, and avoid clock-watching as much as you can. Make a to-do list – even if the only things you manage to tick off are 'eat sandwich', 'watch a bit of Netflix' and 'buy more super-cute sleepsuits online' – and you'll feel like you're whiling the time away until you can get your head down again, or until someone else appears to hold the baby for a bit. Everyone likes ticking off to-dos, right?

5. All the caffeine and sugar

Nobody gets by on kale smoothies and love alone. Man-made energy boosts exist for a reason. Don't overdo it so much that you crash and burn, but allow yourself some treats to perk you up. Happy mum, happy baby? We were thinking more 'happy tum, happy mum'.

WHAT OUR MUM MATES SAY

Don't listen to other mums when they say their babies are already sleeping through the night! It's normal for it to be up and down – you have a good run of nights and you think you've cracked it, and then it all goes wrong again because something else is happening – sleep regressions, teething, constipation when they start on solids, figuring out how to crawl – so the important thing is to accept that babies are babies and not waste too many hours reading blogs and forums about how to get your baby to sleep better.

Jess, mum of one

I was once so tired I accidentally cleaned all my furniture with oven cleaner. Initially I was thinking 'woah, this is the best cleaner ever!' but somehow it took three or four big items of furniture before I realised what I'd done. The moral of the story: don't clean.

Ellie, mum of three

Being a mum in ye olden days vs being a mum now

You'll know by now that older people – mainly mums, aunties and in-laws – just love telling you how they used to do things when they were new mums. You will learn to block most of this out while singing 'Twinkle Twinkle Little Star' very loudly in your own head, but sometimes it's worth

tuning in, because some of their anecdotes are quite entertaining . . . in fact, some might even be helpful.

They left the pram outside in all seasons because it made you nap like a dream

You are too paranoid about someone (what, like one of the
snails that live in your garden?) kidnapping your baby to
leave them unattended, so they mostly nap on or around
you, especially when they're tiny. Nevertheless, you do get
the gist – your baby *does* tend to sleep better when it's had a
bit of fresh air.

They weaned you at six weeks/twelve weeks/while you were still in the womb

You follow modern guidelines to introduce solids from
six months, maybe five and a half if you're feeling really
daring. Your elders might tell you that food will help your
baby sleep better, but this is a myth – milk, whether from
boob or bottle, is far more calorie-rich and nutritious than
a bit of pureed carrot or cardboardy baby rice. It doesn't
help that the four-month sleep regression is very, very real
and totally unrelated to what they eat – the oldies might
well insist this is a sign your baby is gagging for solids,
but actually, it's more likely to make it worse, since their
tummies have a lot of adjusting to do once solids are in the
picture.

They bunged you in a playpen when they needed to get stuff done

You resist buying a playpen, but unwittingly use various modern versions, like ball pools and Jumperoos, which serve the exact same purpose – stopping your baby from flailing around all over the place so that you can Get Shit Done (sorry, Mum), while looking a little bit less like a tiny prison cell.

They drank booze and maybe even smoked while pregnant

You know better. You might well have the odd cheeky glass of wine when you're pregnant (if, of course, you can stomach it), but this is one scenario where modern science has proved that your mum definitely doesn't know best.

They put you to sleep on your front and you consequently slept through the night when you were a minute old

You follow the advice to put your baby to sleep flat on their back, in a cot empty of bumpers and cuddly toys. It's true that babies on their tummies often sleep more deeply – but it's just not worth the risk. Since 1992, when the official guidelines changed and parents were advised to put their little ones on their backs, deaths from SIDS have dropped by 50 per cent. But don't panic if, after a few months, your baby starts to gravitate towards their side or tummy – once they're strong enough to get into the position, they're strong enough to get out of it too.

They tried not to hold or cuddle you too much, because they didn't want to 'spoil' you

You cuddle your baby as much as you damn well please because, guess what, they're a baby and you love them. And funnily enough, Granny seems pretty keen on cuddling them a lot too ...

WHAT OUR MUM MATES SAY

My mum couldn't get her head round baby-led weaning. She was so worried my little one would choke and thought it was completely stupid; she even made up a load of puree for us because she was so worried and thought I was being lazy! I guess it's because she'd done the solids thing so much earlier when we were little – of course, there's no way you'd give a bread roll or a whole banana to a three-month-old!

Mary, mum of two

My granny loves telling me she'd put whisky on her children's gums when they were teething. I have pointed out that there are modern medicines that have the same numbing effect, but she's insistent. I don't think she realises Bonjela is a lot cheaper than whisky too ...

Jo, mum of one

Why your post-baby body is just great, thanks

Never forget: *you made a human*. Of course you don't look exactly the same as you did when you were seventeen, it would be weird if you did. And you wore that awful shimmery eyeshadow then too, remember? But everyone feels insecure about their bodies after popping a baby out – and it doesn't help when we're bombarded with images of celebrities in bikinis while the umbilical cord's practically still attached. What can we do to make it easier?

The insecurity: your mum tum

Ah, the dreaded mum tum. There's no avoiding it. OK, so some new mums 'ping back' pretty quickly – particularly if you were well fit to start with – but, for most of us, it's a bit of a battle. First up, give yourself a break. You're in the middle of a huge transition, and this isn't the time for crash diets or boot camps. But, if you think that getting active will make

you feel better, there are loads of opportunities for new mums to do this with babies in tow – buggy walks, mum and baby yoga or Pilates, dance classes where you can flail around with your baby in a sling ... and they're all a great chance to get out and meet people too. If you're more of a solo exerciser, consider investing in a running buggy (there are always tons available second-hand, and they're often in pretty slick condition since they don't get used very often – babies have a funny way of interfering with exercise routines) and set yourself free! Even if the mum tum is stubborn to shift, those mysterious endorphins will make you feel better about everything.

The insecurity: you don't know what to wear

It doesn't get talked about that much, but lots of new mums go through a huge style crisis. The old you probably had a certain look, a look that might well feel unsuitable now you're a mum – whether it's because the pencil skirts and heels you used to rock in the office on a daily basis simply aren't practical when you're rifling through a changing bag for a missing dummy, or because you suddenly feel 'too old' to be wearing head-to-toe Topshop (which, by the way, is nonsense – you look fahbulous). Plus, you've been in maternity gear for the past few months, so you can't even remember what kind of clothes you actually like anymore. We'd recommend heading to a clothes swap (or even organising one yourself, if you're so inclined) to get new gear – or just new ideas – without spending money. Or, if you really want a whole new look, beg for shopping vouchers for your birthday or Christmas and then throw them at a personal shopper. Yeah, it sounds like something your mum might do but *you're a mum now too.*

The insecurity: you don't recognise your boobs anymore

A lot of people think it's breastfeeding that defaces your boobs, but actually most of the damage is done in pregnancy – sorry about that. It's a sad fact of life that boobs go south as we get older, and, unless you bite the bullet and get surgery, there's very little you can do about it. Getting fitted – properly – for a new bra will help, as will – bear with us, this might sound a bit weird – looking at photos online of 'real' boobs since the variety is far more diverse than we see in mainstream media. Also, pay attention to your partner – chances are they still think your boobs are proper lush.

The insecurity: your, y' know, bits

Even the smoothest of births can make you feel funny about your fanny for months or even years afterwards. And even mums who've had C-sections still suffer with their pelvic floors since, once again, it's blimmin' pregnancy that does a lot of the damage. We all know we're supposed to do pelvic floor exercises, but actually remembering is another matter, especially when we're so fricking busy all the time. There are, naturally, reminder apps for this though, so get one! Also, just give it time and don't put yourself under pressure to get back on the horse – you know, the one who got you into this mess in the first place – before you're ready.

The insecurity: your war wounds

Whether it's a C-section scar or stretch marks where there used to be smooth, taut skin, you might feel super-conscious of your body, even if the mum tum has deflated (lucky you). As ever, *you birthed a human*, but also, if you happen to be at the beach (again, lucky you!), look around you: apart from the nineteen-year-olds frolicking around, feigning an interest in volleyball, the majority of women over thirty or so have evidence of babies about their bodies. You'll get your confidence back soon enough and barely notice the 'damage' – but, until then, high-waisted bikinis flatter everyone and will cover up the bits you're most conscious of.

The insecurity: all of the above

If your self-esteem has really hit rock bottom, and you hate what you see in the mirror, you should talk to someone. If your partner doesn't get it, your mum mates will – chances are they're going through a lot of the same feelings too, even if it's not as intensely as you. But consider talking to your doctor too; feeling super-low about your appearance can be a big part of depression and anxiety. The more you talk about it and tackle it, the sooner you'll be feeling like your old self again.

WHAT OUR MUM MATES SAY

I, like most mums, I expect, optimistically thought I'd be back in my skinny jeans after a few weeks. No chance! Still no, seven months later. But that's totally OK. One thing I have had to figure out though is a new style. My old look made the most of my tiny waist – high-waisted jeans, dresses that went in at the waist, etc. None of that is happening any longer so I've had to come to terms with the fact that (at least for now) I'm going to have to change things up.

Jess, mum of one

I struggled with not finding a way to exercise when becoming a mum, especially in the winter. Then a mum friend with similar interests tipped me off about online fitness videos, which was a game changer. It was a quick way to feel more active without leaving the house, plus my baby found it pretty entertaining to watch me leaping around first thing in the morning.

Katie, mum of two

Things you've realised you no longer have time for now you're a mum

It might take you forty-seven minutes, rather than seconds, to leave the house these days and you might sometimes feel like a frumpy, frazzled mess, but we have good news: now that you're a mum, you're the most efficient you've ever been. Having kids forces you to focus on the things that really matter: you are now the no-frills, best value, most effective version of yourself. But sadly this means there are a few old habits that are now surplus to requirements.

1. Reading novels

When you went on maternity leave, your naive, optimistic self compiled a list of book recommendations; modern must-reads that you visualised yourself devouring while your angelic babe snoozed on your chest. In reality? When the baby's napping, you spend your time tapping: whether you're reading parenting forums, bidding for bargain baby clothes or mindlessly playing games involving colourful pieces of fruit, there are now only two things in your life that can be described as unputdownable: your baby, and your phone. Zadie Smith can wait.

2. Taking your make-up off properly

First things first: you're wearing make-up? It's definitely make-up and not pear puree or wax crayon? Congratulations! The trouble is, on the days when you do find time to smear on a bit of slap, there's absolutely no chance that, when bedtime comes, you'll have time for your old cleanse, tone and moisturise routine. Praise the lord for baby wipes in every room of the house.

3. Keeping up with current events

OK, so the really big stuff still penetrates our conscious-ness (mainly because one thing we *do* find time for is social media) but gone are the days when we could spend hours poring over, and discussing, news and gossip. Don't ask us what's number one in the charts, don't ask us to name more than three global leaders, and please, please, please don't make us try to tell apart any Kardashians. We'll catch up when the kids start school, OK?

4. Tights, fiddly buttons, shoelaces ...

It's during pregnancy that your wardrobe becomes 95 per cent stretchable, breathable fabrics, and it's very difficult to let go of this habit after the baby comes. At first, you're dress-ing for comfort. But soon, you realise those leggings and baggy tops are more practical too – when you have mere sec-onds to go to the loo, you don't want to be fiddling around with tights or unnecessary buttons. Plus, whenever you take your baby to any groups, you'll be expected to remove your shoes while holding your squirming baby, therefore it's flip-flops in summer and slouchy boots in winter.

5. Coordinating bags and coats

On a similar note, remember when you'd idly mull over which bag and coat combo to take to work in order to look stylish, professional and well-prepared? These days, you have one warm, practical, multiple-pocketed coat and one huge, stuffed, filthy bag, both of which you take everywhere without pausing to wonder if they match – you're far too busy trying to find your baby's arm down the sleeve of their infuriating new snowsuit.

6. Sorting the laundry out properly

Back in our single, pre-baby days, when we had a hectic social life, we'd complain that we never had time to do laundry. It's only when you have a baby – who, by the way, will grow up into an even filthier child – that you realise how wrong you were. There's no such thing as dark loads and white loads and delicate loads anymore – these days we just shove the whole lot in and hope that somebody remembers to take it out of the machine before it starts to stink. And once it's dry, does it get put away? Never. Why would we bother doing that when we're only going to wear it again? Oh, and apparently there's also this thing called an iron? Nope, no idea.

7. Three-course meals

'Starter or pudding?' is no longer a question that exists in your universe. In the event that you get out for a meal, instead it's 'Which main course will come the fastest and be easiest to eat with one hand when there's a squawking infant on my lap?'

8. Paperwork

When we have a child-free day, do we go to a spa, a bar, the cinema? Nah, we usually find ourselves catching up on our personal admin. There is no 'I've just had a baby so I'm being a bit slack' box on the tax return form, but there totally should be and we'd totally start a petition about it if we had the time.

WHAT OUR MUM MATES SAY

I used to be pretty well-read so I was gutted to discover that keeping up with modern fiction is pretty impossible when you have a new baby. It's only now that my baby is a toddler that I've got back into it – by joining a library, which doubles up as an activity we can enjoy together since he likes picking out new books too.

Abby, mum of one

Quite often I'm shocked when I realise various celebrities and public figures are dead, but when I look at the date it happened it all suddenly makes sense!

Jo, mum of one

How to take your baby on holiday without losing your mind

There will come a time when you'll feel physically, emotionally and financially ready to go on holiday with your baby. Ignore the miserable naysayers who reckon it's not really a holiday if you have to take your kids. They have a point, but *ignore them*. Or you'll never go. Instead, follow these tips to guarantee* a stress-free† trip.

1. Pick a sensible destination

For the love of God, make your first trip short-haul. If you know you've got to take your little one to Australia in the near future to visit the damned in-laws/go to a free-spirited pal's wedding/tour the *Neighbours* set, then consider a shorter trip first. Spain is great. So is Skegness.

Also, choose the time of your flight carefully – it's worth paying £20 more for a bit more convenience. Lunchtime flights are good for babies on solids (because stuffing them with food fills at least half an hour) but some people prefer late night/ early morning flights because sleep is more likely. In theory.

2. Don't book a hotel

Mmm, hotels, so chic, so sexy, so utterly impractical with a small person. You need your own catering facilities and you need somewhere separate for the baby to sleep so you don't all have to go to bed at the same time.

Airbnb really need a facility where you can narrow your search to properties that are baby-friendly – and we're not just talking highchairs and lifts. It's only when you become a parent that you realise the importance of king-size or at least reasonably sized beds in holiday accommodation – because,

* this is not legally binding.
† OK, not stress-free, but hopefully the fun bits will outweigh the absolutely bloody unbearable bits.

even if you don't normally co-sleep, you might find yourself with an unexpected bed invader due to the unfamiliar environment. Baths, rather than showers, are also handy, but surprisingly hard to come by around the world, in which case you can improvise with a big sink, bucket, or by taking along an inflatable paddling pool. If in doubt, just ask *loads* of annoying questions.

3. Prep your passport referee

You know how you have to put someone's name down on the passport form in the event that they want to confirm your identity? Well, when it comes to baby passports *they actually bother to contact said person*. So, if time is of the essence, make sure yours isn't trekking around Cambodia at the time.

4. Leave the Jumperoo at home

Sometimes when you just nip to the shops with a baby it feels like you've packed for an eight-week cruise, but try really hard to take the opposite approach to your actual holiday. Because you've been sensible and booked self-catering accommodation as we demanded above, you should be able to wash clothes while you're there. When it comes to other essential baby paraphernalia, just take enough for the first 24 hours and then hit the local supermarket (because it turns out foreign babies wear nappies too – who knew?). You don't need more than a couple of small toys either – your baby will much prefer breaking your sunglasses anyway.

One thing you might want to take is a car seat, as the ones

that car hire companies or cab firms offer are often a bit battered. As for wheels, car seat on pram base is a good space-saving solution or, if your baby's old enough, get a cheapo stroller instead of lugging the monster buggy, then you won't be worrying about it getting trashed on the plane. Better still, just take a sling or back carrier. Woo, free hands!

5. Don't fret about the airport

Taking a baby through an airport is like taking Kim Kardashian through an airport – your baby will be treated like the beautiful, but slightly obnoxious, VIP that you've always known he or she is, and you'll get whisked through special family lanes at every stage (although, if it's the school holidays, everybody's in the bloody family lane, so watch out for that).

Most airlines allow you to bring two big baby items at no extra cost (pram/car seat/travel cot). You have to get tags for these at bag drop and then drag them to the oversized luggage bit. Sneaky tip: get a special bag to stash them in (there are tons of generic buggy bags online) and you can slip in a few extra bits and bobs (nappies/bedding/more frocks for you) without anyone noticing.

6. Arm yourself on the plane (not literally. Definitely, definitely not literally)

Having a wriggly baby on your lap for a whole plane journey, even a short one, is going to be the worst bit of your holiday. Sorry about that.

Some things that will make it more pleasant include: aisle seats (so you can get up and down if your baby is a jiggler) boobs/bottles (milk for baby, wine for mummy), snacks if baby is of a snacking age, eight previously downloaded episodes of your CBeebies fix of choice (now is not the time to implement a screen ban), some small innocuous toys and a positive mental attitude. Also, and this is important, get one of those cute, chilled-out babies that just smiles at everyone. If this is not yours, consider swapping with a friend. Just for the duration of the holiday, mind – we're not monsters.

7. Adjust your baby's body clock

This is easier said than done, but trying to tweak your baby's usual habits so that they turn into a dream Mediterranean baby called Stavros is worth doing. If you're somewhere hot, they'll likely have a long nap in the afternoon anyway so take the opportunity to keep them up later so you can all enjoy dinner together.

Massive generalisation: foreign people adore babies and are much less rude than Brits, so they won't even mind if little Stavros chucks regurgitated bread all over the patio of their charming taverna.

8. Have a good time

The way you holiday has changed for ever (well, for the next fifteen years at least) but that doesn't mean you won't enjoy it. Will you finally get round to reading the pile of books that's been on your bedside table since the last time you ovulated? Probably not, but seeing the amazement on your baby's face as they dip their cute little tootsies into the sea for the first time is better than any book. Enjoy every moment and Instagram the hell out of it.

WHAT OUR MUM MATES SAY

My absolute number one tip for your first holiday is to consider going away with your extended family. This might have sounded like the stuff of nightmares to your old self, but going somewhere with built-in babysitters will mean you might actually feel like you've had a holiday too. We've been away with the grandparents a few times and everybody's loved it – they get to spend time with the kids, we get a tiny bit of downtime, and the little ones get extra attention. It helps that they have a habit of paying for meals too ...

Michelle, mum of two

We went on a short trip to Spain when our baby was about four months old, and I was quite stressed ahead of the plane journey. It was actually totally fine, lots of people cooed over the baby and he was small enough that having him on my lap for three hours was no hassle and he mainly just slept and fed. It's much harder with a toddler who won't keep still!

Izzy, mum of two

6

Six to twelve months

When you've totally got this. Ish.

Wow, that went fast, didn't it? There we go again, spouting those clichés we warned you about. Of course, your baby is still very much a baby, but the days of them being an expressionless fragile little thing whose every bodily function baffles you are long gone.

But now there's just so much to think about. Over the next few months, they'll be starting solids and getting mobile and chances are, the baby bubble is about to burst for you since you might well be contemplating going back to work and all it entails (mainly childcare and clothes other than leggings. Eek). Heck, maybe if you're really brave, you're even thinking about having another baby some time.

While the first few months are pretty similar for most mums, we know that it's around now that things can fragment a little. If you've built up a solid group of mum friends, for instance, they'll probably be gradually drifting back to work, which means those long mornings of drinking coffee together while analysing sleep patterns to death are a distant memory; everyone's getting busy, and the transition can be tough for all sorts of reasons.

You're still on a steep learning curve (turns out that never ends) and could be feeling overwhelmed. If the first months felt surreal, almost like you were playing at being a parent, it's about now that it just becomes a way of life, with your baby influencing every decision you make – and there are a lot to make . . .

Weaning: an emotional rollercoaster

For the first few months of their lives, babies do very little of note (sorry, mums of newborns. Your baby is *utterly adorable* but they're also a bit boring). So when the time comes to give them solids, almost like they're a functioning human rather than a weird little immobile alien, it all feels very exciting indeed. You plan to transform into a domestic goddess, with an adoring, appreciative baby gurgling at you from their highchair while you prepare lavish, perfectly balanced feasts. Unfortunately, this isn't always the reality.

Stage One: Excitement

'I can't wait to get him on solids!' you tell all your mum friends. 'It looks like so much fun!' 'Don't be too excited,' says the wise one with older kids. 'In fact, put it off for as long as possible.' But no: you're adamant that weaning is going to be a total blast. Messy, sure, but what a hoot, what a milestone, what an adventure. Right?

Stage Two: Anticipation

First there will be an IKEA trip, for the obligatory Antilop highchair (and some of those long-sleeved bibs and loads of plastic spoons, and why not buy a new sofa and five hundred tea lights while you're there?).

There will be extensive research, as you pore over the entire works of Annabel Karmel, um and ah over baby-led weaning versus traditional weaning and ultimately decide to just kind of wing it.

And there will be lots and lots of tense conversations with well-meaning older relatives who don't understand why you're waiting until the NHS-advised six months, when they gave their baby a rusk while they were still in the womb and they turned out just fine and slept twenty-eight hours a night at six days old.

Stage Three: The big day

And then the day will come when you'll be ready to introduce that first solid. Into the highchair they go, in their pristine new bib. The kitchen is immaculate for the first time in months too, because God forbid a rogue cloth makes it into the background of the photo you're going to Instagram the hell out of in a few minutes.

Stage Four: The anticlimax

Now here comes the mashed-up pear/sweet potato/nutrition-ally bereft baby rice you've lovingly prepared. Aaaaaand . . . . nothing. Literally no reaction, they've maybe ingested a speck and the rest lies dribbled out (traditional weaning) or discarded (baby-led) in front of them. You share a picture anyway, captioned: 'First taste of real food! He loved it!' Granny replies: 'About time too! Bet he'll sleep well tonight!' followed by some emojis that don't make any sense.

Stage Five: Blind fear

Despite the fact that you have made sure there are no grapes within a three-mile radius of your home, at some point during those first few weeks of weaning your baby is going to gag on something, probably a rogue bit of bread that's gone all gloopy in their useless toothless gob.

You never did get round to that baby first-aid course, so you find yourself frantically searching YouTube for advice. You've only got as far as clammily unlocking your phone when you discover they're now smiling at you while smearing yoghurt into their eyes. Crisis averted. But you revert to gooey food only for the next few days.

Stage Six: Frustration

You're a couple of months in now and Becca from NCT's baby is on three full meals and two healthy snacks a day. Knowing Becca from NCT's baby, he probably cooks them himself.

Meanwhile, your kid still doesn't appear to have absorbed more than a few crumbs, apart from when you admitted defeat and gave them a shop-bought pouch, which they devoured.

Stage Seven: Disgust

Right, so they're eating OK now, but *flipping heck, what is that in their nappy*? A cinnamon stick? Relax, it's normal. Grim, but normal. It will sort itself out. In the meantime, you experiment with twenty-seven different types of sippy cup to try to get them to drink more water.

Stage Eight: Guilt

You cannot believe how much food is being wasted every day. Weetabix glued to the floor, pasta bakes you spent hours preparing festering by the sink with only 2.5 mouthfuls consumed, piles and piles of fruit rotting in the bowl because your plans to batch cook and freeze stuff into ice trays are going about as well as the best-selling crime thriller you vowed to write on maternity leave. 'Just give them whatever you're having!' say your friends when you complain, seemingly unaware that you exist on a diet of Hobnobs, Cup-a-Soups and frozen pizza.

Stage Nine: Realisation

So, seriously, this is it now, making sure this kid gets fed three times a day is actually your responsibility for the next eighteen years? And probably a few more years after that because they're not going to be able to leave home until they're thirty-eight (#politics)? Man alive, this is tedious. Why didn't you just listen to your mate with all the kids?

WHAT OUR MUM MATES SAY

My husband was so stubborn – despite everyone recommending the cheap Ikea highchair, he went off and bought a massive, cushioned one that took up most of the kitchen and made my daughter look like some kind of mafia Don! It got ridiculous so he buckled and went to Ikea – lesson learned!

Claire, mum of two

With my first, I diligently prepared purees and froze them, baked healthy muffins and generally treated weaning like it was a PhD. Second time round I think their first meal was beans on toast. They're both fine.

Jen, mum of two

I was beside myself that my daughter didn't poo for days after first going on to solids. Despite being reassured it was completely normal, I got extremely over-excited when her first 'proper food' poo arrived. I went to take a picture of said poo in her nappy, but managed to let it roll, from a considerable height, on to my bedroom carpet in front of my horrified mum. I still have the photo though!

Jo, mum of one

Teething: frequently asked questions (especially at 4.13 am)

Are amber beads total woo? Why does he suddenly have green poo? When will this hell end? And some more sensible ones ...

How do I know if my baby is definitely teething?

It's a tricky one. There's always a chance that your baby is just a terrible person. But, generally, if they're between one minute and seventy-eight years old, and exhibiting more than two or three of the following symptoms, they're probably teething.

- Waterfall of saliva pouring from their gobs (dribble bibs are a godsend and look pretty hipster)
- Massive red cheeks that totally clash with their outfit
- An unsightly runny nose (said dribble bibs double up as seriously grim snotty hankies)
- Uniquely disgusting poo (yes, even worse than usual)
- Disrupted sleep (as opposed to the twelve unbroken hours of blissed-out slumber we all normally get, right?)
- Constant, seemingly irrational whinging (probably them *and* you)
- Shoving anything they can get their chubby little hands on into their mouths, including their chubby hands themselves
- And yet, rejecting actual food. You know, the thing they're supposed to put in their mouth.

But don't be thinking all this means your baby's going to get some cute little peggies soon. That would be too easy. This nonsense takes months. Plenty of babies enjoy putting inanimate objects into their mouths (phone chargers, takeaway fliers, the cat), appear to have visible tooth buds or at least sharper gums than before from when they're very wee and start sporadically acting like prize arseholes from, ooh, birth, but don't get any actual teeth for MONTHS. Then they'll probably go and cut four in a fortnight. Fun times. They do look cute though.

What are these amber bead thingies?

Noticed that a lot of one-year-olds look like they've just got back from a gap year backpacking around Southeast Asia? Well, those beaded necklaces you see so many red-faced little terrors wearing aren't just a fashion statement, they're teething aids. Maybe.

There are two types of mother: those who believe in the powers of amber to provide pain relief to their drooling beast, and those who are just too embarrassed to look like they believe in the powers of amber to provide pain relief to their drooling beast.

In theory, the succinic acid in the amber acts as a natural painkiller, absorbed by their lovely warm skin and sending some sort of happy hippy zippy zaps towards their teeth. In practice, this is scientifically impossible. Plus, they're not actually very safe: choking hazard, strangulation hazard, all that jazz. But hey, if it gets you through the day, proceed with caution.

So, what does help then?

Moaning about it to your mum friends helps. Oh, you mean what helps the baby? Pfft. Bonjela, Calpol, those powders that make you feel like you're doing recreational drugs with your baby are all worth a go ... but they'll probably prefer sleeping in your bed and gnawing your boobs.

Why did ten different friends give me a rubber giraffe when the baby was born?

Sophie la Girafe is a popular overpriced teething aid. Like a middle-class dog toy. Everyone has one. Wait, everyone has four. Some mums like to proffer them to their offspring in an exaggerated French accent: 'Finlay, would you like to play with Soh-fee lah jeeeeghraf now?' making you wonder if Finlay has red cheeks because he's teething, or just embarrassed by his mum.

Why is teething worse at night?

Because everything is worse at night.

Does teething really cause an upset tummy?

Some people say there is no evidence of this. These people are liars. Lots of babies do weird, explosive, mucusy poos (and even vomit) when they're teething because of all that drool they're swallowing. It makes total sense, but it's grim. You'll think they have a terrible bug (obviously if you *really* think this, then see a doctor) and then, lo and behold, a few days later a pesky little tooth pokes through and the flow of grossness abruptly stops.

So, beware, if you are #blessed with a spewy teether, it's back to those newborn habits of carrying seventeen muslins, three changes of clothes (for you and them), a range of carpet-cleaning implements and an apologetic face.

When should I start brushing their teeth?

It's good to form this habit early, and baby toothbrushes are also dead cute. So, once a tooth or two has broken through, try to start brushing (using the teeniest smear of baby toothpaste – you can just dab the bristles in the top of the tube) once or twice a day. Do yours at the same time because your baby has an unsophisticated sense of humour and will find it flipping hilarious.

When will this hell end?

Generally, it slows down a bit once the first few are through, although gets nasty again when they're two-ish and their back molars do their thing.

And then, in a few years, those teeth, those evil teeth that caused so much pain, will only go and fall out and cost the tooth fairy* *actual money*. What a bloody waste of time and energy all that was.

---

* You. You're the tooth fairy. As if you didn't have enough roles already.

WHAT OUR MUM MATES SAY

Every time my little boy was in a bad mood I'd blame it on teething. He actually didn't get his first tooth until he was over eleven months, so I'm not sure those meltdowns when he was five months can really be excused with it. It's a good catch-all excuse when you're embarrassed by your baby screaming out and about though!

Izzy, mum of two

Some people worry about breastfeeding when their baby starts getting teeth, but honestly, it's rarely an issue. If your baby does get a bit bitey, they'll soon lay off when they realise you abruptly stop feeding every time they do it ...

Luisa, mum of one

How to have a social life and keep your old friends happy

It's hard to keep on top of your social life when your most high-maintenance little friend of all is consuming your mind, body and bank balance.

Having a kid is awesome. People who say they love every minute of it are liars/loons, but, despite the four-month sleep regression; hand, foot and mouth disease; leaky boobs and other delights, most mums are pretty pleased with their baby.

However ... life is never the same again. Especially your

social life. You'll go around telling people you 'used to be fun' while wondering what happened.

If you have friends with babies around the same age, your daytime fun is sorted, at least for the first few months. In those hazy newborn days, you'll hugely value anyone who's around to inhale chocolate chip cookies and pace the park with you.

So daytimes are all good. And evenings will be spent at home, taking it in turns to heat up food and eat dinner. Having a night-time social life will probably feel like an impossibility for quite some time, but there are things you can do to make the gulf between you and your old life a bit less ravine-like.

1. Organise stuff

When you first have a baby, everyone turns up bearing baby-gros and cheap fizz, but then it stops and they get on with their enriching careers and vibrant social lives, while you stay in and learn the difference between Pinky Ponk and Ninky Nonk. The onus is on you to organise stuff, or they'll assume you don't have time for them.

The issue here is lack of compatibility. They're at work all day, you're not. They go out in the evening, you can't (because the baby won't take a bottle) or you don't want to (so you pretend the baby won't take a bottle). Stop moaning and just go and meet your friends for lunch near their work – seriously, it's *so* much easier with a portable little baby who's not yet in a routine than it is when they're older.

And if you really can't be arsed, then for God's sake, invite people over for dinner or a weekend lunch. You don't need to wear make-up. With some friends, you don't even need to wear clothes.

2. Show an interest in other people's lives

Your pre-baby self probably whinged incessantly about how much people banged on about their tedious babies. But then it transpired that your baby was the most interesting baby to ever have been born, and you understood, right? But ... your non-mum friends won't understand. They love you, and they mostly tolerate your baby, but remember to ask them about that boss they hate/play they're writing/bloke they're shagging. Also, try to post things other than photos of your baby on Facebook. Occasionally.

3. Don't put pressure on yourself

The first couple of times you go out in the evening post-baby, you might not enjoy it at all. If the highlight of your evening is finding out that your Uber driver has a baby born *the same month, what a coincidence* as yours, you know it's probably too soon – you are officially still in the new-baby bubble and not ready to wear a wired bar or queue up for overpriced drinks in bars full of nubile twenty-three-year-olds. You'll want to be at home talking about and/or staring at the world's best baby. Or just getting some sleep.

This is OK. There is no huge rush; there will always be overpriced drinks. If you wait until you're ready, you'll be better company than when your boobs are crying and you're checking your phone every three seconds. For some people, this is after nine days. For others, nine months. For some, nine years.

4. Don't be flaky

You think you don't have time to reply to that lovely email from your crazy old workmate, but you do – you're just choosing to use your precious three minutes of downtime to do other stuff.

Social media can make us feel connected to people we don't often see, which is great. But we also use it as an excuse to not actually *be* connected with people we like ('Seen Mel recently?', 'Yes, of course! I mean, on Facebook . . . ').

What often happens is that messages come from friends when you're in the middle of something (poo), so then you forget to reply promptly. And then you feel awkward about it. It's time to take the approach you would with other crucial life admin and start making lists of people you need to get in touch with – because keeping up with people you think are awesome is just as important as remembering to buy bathroom cleaner.

5. Make time for the other love of your life too

It takes a while to feel confident leaving your precious first-born in the care of another for an evening, so for months, or even years, you might feel like you've vaguely got your social life back, but actually it's only 50 per cent of it, because you and your partner take it in turns to go out.

This means, all of 'his' friends (who you love too. Well,

most of them) only get to see him, because he gets custody of those invitations, while you just end up on girls' nights. With other mums. Talking about your babies.

While you might book a babysitter/grandmother several months in advance for a wedding or other big do, you really miss those spontaneous trips to the pub after work with your beloved. Try to plan childcare for a couple of more low-key nights too. Or just buy a house next door to a pub and get a really good baby monitor. (Obviously this is a joke. Nobody can afford to move house when they've just had a baby . . .)

WHAT OUR MUM MATES SAY

After I had my daughter I finally got it – why my friends with kids didn't come out as much as they used to. I felt really guilty for ever judging them. I had this stupid idea that everything would be the same after having a baby, including my social life. I used to love going out a lot and I never anticipated how I would lose the inclination to, and obviously be too shattered to a lot of the time. Sadly a few friendships have dwindled since having a baby but I feel I have changed too. On my first and probably last big night out post baby I fell down some stairs and dislocated my shoulder!

Ru, mum of one

I've taken a breast pump on a hen do, and had to fire it up in the ladies loos, and I've also rolled in after one too many cocktails to a baby wanting a late-night feed. All in all, having babies has actually helped my social life. We didn't know anyone in our area, but now we feel firmly part of the community.

Claire, mum of two

My first night away without my little boy was at only 14 weeks as I had promised my friend that a night away for her hen do was going to be no problem at all ... Little did I realise I would be totally knackered (what with a baby who was waking every two hours) and not really up for drinking loads. Having to 'pump yourself' in front of childless people isn't the most glamorous thing to do whilst the others are applying false lashes and bronzer! At least I'd have a full night's undisturbed sleep, right? Wrong. There were three of us in two double beds so some bright spark suggested we push them together. Obviously I was the one who ended up in the middle and came home even more tired than normal!

Anna, mum of one

Adventures in choosing childcare

When you've recently had a baby, people will relentlessly ask you what the plan is re: 'work'. What they're really asking is: do you still give a damn about your career or do you prefer 'Row Row Row Your Boat?'

Whether you want to keep your precious firstborn nestled to your bosom for ever or can't wait to get the hell back to work, choosing childcare is *hard*. There are so many options, and none of them will seem good enough for The Best And Most Important Baby Ever. But, if The Best And Most Important Baby Ever wants to continue to wear clothes, play with toys and have a roof over its head, chances are you will need an income at some point. So, what do you do? Here's a rundown of the most popular three options (we haven't included au pairs, since they're generally for school-age kids, and we haven't included your baby's grandparents, because we've never met them).

Nursery pros

- All the boring but important stuff: they're generally open fifty-one weeks a year, everything – food, hygiene, learning – is very regulated, and the staff have lots of certificates which you pretend to know the meaning of when you look around: 'Oh, a Level Eighteen GQWTF in Sensory Waterplay and Montessori Sandpittery With Merit? Brilliant, that's a real priority for us as a family, where do we sign up?'
- Generally, an economical option. Obviously, all childcare is extortionate unless you've got willing grandparents, but nurseries are cheaper than nannies, and often on a par with childminders.
- The kids get to 'socialise'. OK, so most kids socialise plenty whatever their childcare arrangements, but seeing them play with other little ones in the same age in a neutral environment (rather than having turf wars over pieces of Lego) is nice.

Nursery cons

- If your kid is sick, the nursery won't want them there. And they will get sick, a lot, because they're suddenly licking the same toys as twenty other Arlo's and Orla's. You and your partner will then have a hideous argument about whose job is most important.
- Fixed hours. Fine if you've got a nine to five, not so handy if you're one of those trendy self-employed types. And you *will* be penalised if your train is delayed (or you went for a quick one after work).
- Long waiting lists. Some people go and look at nurseries before they've even changed the conception bedsheets. Waiting list scare-mongering is rife. Don't panic: places come up more often than you think. But it is a good idea to go and have a look while your baby's quite little.

Childminder pros

- Home-from-home environment. Want your child to have access to home-cooked food and cuddles while never missing an episode of *This Morning* in a room that smells just ever so slightly of wee? Then childminders are the way forward. OK, this is unfair, many of them have a set-up as slick and well-equipped as a top nursery, but they're still more homely and (slightly) less shrill.
- More bonding opportunities. Your precious babe will get to know one carer, as opposed to dozens of nursery staff. There will be fewer kids too, which is a big plus for children of a nervous and/or attention-seeking disposition.

- Usually the cheapest option – but flexible too. Lots of them do half days (handy for anyone who often shirks from home), they don't mind if you're a bit swappy with your days and will generally look after your child even if they're sick.

Childminder cons

- Good ones are hard to find – and highly sought after. Word of mouth is the way forward.
- Although childminders are good at taking their brood out and about, your babba will also likely be dragged along on multiple school pick-ups and could get overshadowed by rowdy older kids. Also, many – but not all – childminders operate term-time only. Great if you're a teacher though.

Nanny pros

- Fancy yourself as a bit posh? Like the idea of casually dropping the words 'my darling nanny Maria is a whizz with quinoa' into conversation? Then this option will appeal to your ego. Only the best for little snookums.
- You don't have to worry about drop-offs, pick-ups or getting your little one fed and dressed before you go to work. In fact, a good nanny won't care if the entire family are wearing only a thin layer of pear puree when she (or he, if you hired a lesser-spotted manny) arrives, because she is paid (pretty well) to deal with this mess.

- Major bonding. Between baby and nanny, that is, not between spouse and nanny (this only happens in Hollywood, and your husband isn't even the best-looking man in the IT department, so don't worry about it).

Nanny cons

- Expensive. But this is where another great option – the nanny share – comes in. If you have a like-minded and conveniently located mum friend with similar childcare needs, sharing a nanny only costs a few quid more than nursery and is dead handy – not to mention more sociable than the solo option, for those still obsessed with turning their child's early years into one long freshers' week.
- More admin. Any decent nanny will need to be properly employed by you, meaning you pay their tax and NI on top of their wage (there are lots of companies who deal with the paperwork for you though).
- It's less regulated than the other options. When interviewing nannies, you'll find a mixture of disillusioned nursery workers seeking a way out, free-wheelin' creatives looking to supplement their passion (acting/painting/ getting to the final twelve on *X Factor*) with a steady part-time job, plus career nannies, who will fulfil all your Mrs Doubtfire dreams, but likely cost the most. The dream nanny will have all the certificates *and* wow you with their vibrant personality and promises of puppet shows in seven languages, but they're tough to find, and going through agencies can be pricier still.

WHAT OUR MUM MATES SAY

I work freelance so committing to childcare was really tricky. What if we paid for set days and then I didn't have any work? Or what if I got loads of work when we didn't have any childcare? It's really tough to work out what to do and there's a severe lack of flexible options. I felt really jealous of friends who had their mums round the corner, willing to drop everything!

Lucy, mum of one

We met some really 'interesting' characters when interviewing for nannies. There was one who rescheduled her interview to later in the day, claiming a family emergency, but then turned up bright orange, with that weird biscuity smell, clearly straight from the tanning salon, one who listed all her pets on her CV and another one who I found naked pictures of when I did a very quick google. We got a bit worried that there were no normal nannies out there but in the end we found an amazing one!

Izzy, mum of two

The nine stages of going back to work

When the time comes to hand your baby over to someone or other who seems trustworthy and go back to earning a living, you will have seriously mixed emotions. You know you'll miss your precious offspring with all your heart, but you'll also feel excited about being you again. Having kids can also really help clarify what you do and don't want from work. You won't have the brain space to get as bogged down with office politics and will feel like a proper grown-up. This might make you more awesome than ever at your job – or it might make you question everything and embark on a whole new career. But whatever line of work you're in, there will be a few common themes.

1. 'I'm ready . . . '

It's like the ultimate back-to-school feeling (er, especially if you happen to be a teacher). You might even have a new pencil case, or perhaps a new bag (because all your old ones are full of rice cakes, baby wipes and despair). You'll massively over-prepare, planning your first day outfit, your first day lunch and your first day commute until every second of your day is accounted for. And you'll be excited, but nervous too. What if you've forgotten how to do your job? What if they liked your maternity cover more than you? What if they've moved the toilets?

2. 'I'm not ready!'

Then reality hits. You've got to do your job *and* factor in the new routine of your baby. Pre-procreation, you used to idly spend an hour or two getting ready in the morning, sipping tea, taking in a bit of breakfast telly and straightening your hair, but now you'll be lucky to have thirty seconds to brush your teeth. Tense negotiations will take place with your partner over pick-ups, drop-offs, nappies, breakfast ... it's like starting this parenting business all over again. *How do people do it?*

3. 'I've got this'

A day or two in, you are Living the Dream. Hot drinks at your desk, delicious grown-up lunches from the new place around the corner, which is noticeably lacking in highchairs and crayons, wees whenever you want them (well, unless you're stuck in an unbearable meeting) and best of all, *adult conversation*. Speaking of which ...

4. 'Oh God, I'm so boring ... '

Then it dawns on you: all you do is talk about your baby. And show people photos of your baby. You have become That Person. But what the hell else are you supposed to talk about? You make a mental note to watch some topical TV shows so you can bring them up and pretend to be someone who has a life outside of CBeebies.

5. 'I miss them'

The first week or two back at work feels a bit like a holiday. It's only when you realise that this is it now, you are a working mum and will be for the foreseeable future – say, forty years, give or take another maternity leave or two – that reality bites. The juggle is real. And you feel sad that you're no longer the person your baby spends most of their time with. So, you book a load of annual leave and start planning some holidays.

6. 'Am I taking the piss?'

If you've negotiated a shorter week, or reduced hours, so you can actually see the adorable little person you love most in the world for more than a stressy minute a day, you'll have a horrible cocktail of guilt swirling around in your stomach. You're convinced your full-time, non-parent colleagues will think you're a good-for-nothing skiver, but you'll also feel guilty for being away from your baby at all. The truth is, most working parents massively over-compensate for these feelings and work harder than they ever have before. Plus, you should never forget that if you've managed to wangle some flexibility with your employer, they obviously highly value you. So swallow that guilt along with the overpriced sushi you just wolfed down at your desk because you're too scared to take more than nine minutes for lunch.

7. 'Uh oh, I'm drunk'

The first time you go for after-work drinks is quite the mile-stone. Not only does it mean that you won't see your baby before they go to bed, but it also means your colleagues are about to witness your newly lightweight self drinking white wine spritzers – the mum drink of choice – on an empty stomach. *Mum on the razz alert.* Except you, of course, spend the first part of the evening talking about your baby with long-suffering Jacqui from HR, and the last part ... you're not sure ... but you're pretty sure the post room guy gave you a shot of something aniseedy? For the first time, you're glad you've got work the next day – work on a hangover is *way* more bearable than looking after a baby when you have a hangover.

8. 'I'm rich!'

That first pay cheque after months of statutory maternity pay will make you feel rich beyond your wildest dreams – and like a real functioning adult again. But don't get too excited and blow it on ridiculous shoes because ...

9. 'WTF?'

... when the childcare fees have come out, you'll wonder why you bothered.

WHAT OUR MUM MATES SAY

Remember, it's OK to want to work! I actually prefer being at work most of the time even though I adore my daughter. Coupled with that is obviously a massive amount of guilt that I am not enthralled by every waking moment with her or desperate to do crafty stuff and play mindless games.

Katherine, mum of one

Most of the women in my family have stayed at home until the kids have started school, so I felt like I was being judged when I went back to work and it took a while for me to feel properly ready. Of course, this wasn't true at all – everyone understands that most modern couples can't survive on one salary, and the breadwinner + housewife model is seriously outdated. Plus, as much as I love being a mum, I worked hard for fifteen years before having kids and my career is a big part of my identity – even when I'm sweatily racing from office to nursery after another delayed train, I wouldn't give it up.

Michelle, mum of two

I loved the first few months with my little girl. A roller-coaster obviously, but the highs are magic, and maternity leave is also amazing when you have good people to spend it with. I'm starting to go back to work now and it's sad to think that mat leave is coming to an end but it also does feel good to be using my brain and doing something other than childcare 24/7!

Jess, mum of one

And why it's OK to *not* go back to work

Sometimes you're still wearing maternity pads when people start asking about your plans to return to work. And it can be tough to talk about it – no matter how much you love your job, when you're in the middle of the baby bubble, it's impossible to think about weekly catch-ups and KPIs and what's the name of that guy in the sandwich shop again? Yep, your old life suddenly feels a million miles away from your new reality of nappies and night feeds and nipple cream.

But maternity leave trundles along and suddenly going to work isn't such an abstract concept anymore. For many mums, there's no decision to be made – you've committed to taking six or nine or twelve months off work, and that is what you'll do, because you have to and/or because you want to.

But it's not always as simple as that. Making the decision to not go back to work and be a stay-at-home mum is a big one, and it can make you feel like you're on your own. However, there are loads of scenarios that spur people into making the exact same choice – even if it doesn't feel like one.

You can't afford to go back to work

Many mums realise that, once childcare and travel are factored in, going back to work just isn't a financial option – which can make you feel trapped, especially if all the other mums you met on maternity leave are now swanning around with takeaway coffee and wearing actual make-up. While it used to be the norm for women to assume the role of 'housewife' until the kids started school – or even longer – it's pretty unusual these days, so you can feel pretty lonely.

If you're in this boat, no matter how much you love your baby, it can feel like there's no end in sight. Giving yourself projects that you can do around your baby – a blog, a small business, or just taking up a new hobby – can stop you feeling like your brain's turning to, well, mush, and potentially inspire plans for when childcare is more viable (and paid for!). And remember, there's a lot of 'grass is greener' going on when it comes to all this – your mum mates who are dashing around from commute to nursery pick-up would love to be in your shoes sometimes.

You can afford to not go back to work

If not going back to work is a choice you and your partner have made because they earn enough to support the whole family and you're quite happy to be a stay-at-home mum, there can still be challenges. Depending on the kind of area you live in, there might be lots of SAHMs knocking around, or you might be unusual, but it can still be a major mental adjustment. When people ask you what you do for a living, for instance, you can feel embarrassed – especially if you've put a high-flying career on hold to do the baby thing. But, remember, the choice you've made is an admirable one – after all, we all know that looking after kids is WAY harder and more exhausting than most other jobs ...

You need a change of direction

If maternity leave made you realise just how much you hated your job, you may have taken the opportunity to tell your boss where they can shove it (in the career listings section of the company website, obvs – what else could we mean?). So, it seems you're now a stay-at-home mum, even if you're not planning to stay that way for very long. Plotting your next move can be tricky when every day revolves around your baby, so, if it's an option, consider calling in favours or paying for a few hours of childcare a week so you can focus on you, you, you. If you've got a mum friend in a similar situation, you could take it in turns to look after each other's kids while you polish your CVs, set up meetings or learn some new skills.

Your kid has additional needs

This is the one that can turn life upside down the most. If your baby has health or developmental issues, going back to work might be a total impossibility, and that can be hugely challenging to deal with for a multitude of reasons. If this is you, make sure you're getting all the help you're entitled to – both financially and when it comes to practical and emotional support – and seek out mum friends in the same circumstances. You might not see them in every coffee shop, but we promise they're out there.

WHAT OUR MUM MATES SAY

I stayed at home until my youngest started school, because my husband just about earned enough to support us, and at the time I felt like my career was going nowhere. We had to be very careful with money for those early years and I did sometimes feel lonely, but having that time with the kids when they were tiny was lovely, and now they're all going through school, I am working full-time again in a whole new field and absolutely loving it. It really helped focus me on what I really wanted to do.

Michelle, mum of three

Going back to work wasn't really financially viable, but I knew I'd get bored if I was doing mum stuff 24/7, so, after the first few months, I spent my evenings and all of her naps retraining via a course directed at mums looking for flexibility. It made me feel a lot better about the fact that all the local mums I knew had gone back to work. Now my little girl goes to nursery a couple of days a week and I do freelance work around this. It's a brilliant balance for us and I don't miss my old job at all.

Lou, mum of one

I do sometimes feel embarrassed telling new people I'm a stay-at-home mum – they seem to assume I'm either getting by on benefits, or hugely privileged with a rich husband, when the reality is definitely somewhere in between! But I love my time with my little ones, and that makes it all worth it. Every family just has to make the right decision for them, we're all different!

Jen, mum of two

How to eat out with a baby without making everyone hate you

Babies are wonderful for many things, but they're not always the best dinner dates. Sure, they look cute, but their table manners leave a lot to be desired and they almost never offer to split the bill. However, there are a few ways to make the experience more pleasurable for all concerned (even fellow diners ... maybe). Soon, your baby will be able to tell you where to get the best overpriced, microwaved mac and cheese with a side order of crayons – and which stressed mummy haven begrudgingly serves the best babyccino ...

1. Start 'em young

You might think otherwise while you're grappling with one, but four-month-old babies do nothing – literally nothing. So, the best way to get started on your infant culinary odyssey is to go when they're immobile and can be muted with a boob or bottle. If you want to venture out once they're older and can actually eat food themselves, it's probably worthwhile to start them young to get them used to formal-ish dining environments, just like fancy French babies who don't throw food.

2. It's all in the timing

There's only one thing worse than babies in restaurants, and that's tired babies in restaurants. If your little one naps after lunch, like most babies and the entire population of the Mediterranean tend to, you'll want to be impatiently pacing around outside your chosen venue at 11.48 am, ready to burst through the doors, cause a kerfuffle with your buggy and order as close to midday as possible, so you can be out of there before they start flagging.

Doesn't sound relaxing enough for you? Then why not take bubs out for dinner instead? By dinner we mean 5.00 pm. Possibly 4.45 pm. This is a particularly nice thing to do *en famille* at weekends when restaurants and pubs are full to the brim of terrible people like you. And by 'you' I mean 'us'.

3. Think outside the pizza box

Family-orientated chain restaurants are – obviously – great with kids. Pizza Express, Giraffe, Bill's et al. are all equipped with stacks of highchairs, affordable kiddy menus and staff who've been well-trained to pretend they don't hate you.

But, if you're too cool for chains (a delusion many of us experience, until *free crayons*), these aren't the only options. Our mum mates have also reported successful dining experiences at tapas joints (constant flow of food, good chance for your baby to try different things, but they can always fall back on patatas bravas, and – sweeping generalisation – Spanish people love babies so they won't resent you), Chinese restaurants and lots and lots of random pubs. Basically, anywhere with an IKEA Antilop highchair, because sitting them in anything else is overrated.

4. Bring back-up

Once your baby is properly on solids, it's a bit off to bring your own food out with you all the time. Plus, you're eating out – this is a special treat that is ruined if you still have to prepare a flavourless pasta bake that they'll probably throw on the floor. But hors d'ouevres in the form of breadsticks or those cardboardy baby crisps are fine. Essential, in fact, to keep your squawker quiet while you wait for the proper food to arrive. Don't leave the house without them. The breadsticks, that is. The baby is optional, if you've got a good babysitter.

5. In fact, bring everything

The most crucial thing you can bring when dining out with your baby is *all the things*. Items that can provide up to six whole minutes of distraction without being too irritating for fellow diners include Duplo bricks, crayons, felt tips, stickers, your purse, your mobile phone, your sunglasses ... all the crap that you don't let them play with at home, basically. Deploy them gradually so that when there's a hold-up on the fish-finger sandwiches, you can bring out the big guns (your car keys).

6. Order wisely

Mess at home is manageable. But mess in a restaurant can be stressful. If you haven't packed a full-body bib and/or change of clothes (for you *and* them), don't order anything for them involving beans, spaghetti or excessive sauce in general. Far less messy options include fish fingers, pizza, chips, anything bread-based – oh yeah, this isn't a time for 'clean eating' (the time for clean eating with a baby is about three days after hell freezes over, FYI). Bear this in mind when choosing your own meal too, since babies always prefer other people's food to their own.

7. Remember, some people just hate your kid

Some people enjoy tutting and sighing whenever they see anyone under the age of twenty-eight, so certain are they of imminent annoyance. This, quite frankly, is their problem – your baby has just as much right to be whining and dining as everyone else. But miserable old bores are best ignored, so don't bother trying to engage them in a game of peekaboo. Instead, just have a nice time and hopefully annoy them all the more by not actually doing anything to annoy them.

The main annoying thing that little people do in restaurants is move around. How very dare they? But the thing is, while you think they look super-cute toddling through the restaurant, pulling down condiment displays and tripping up waitresses, in reality, even to people who quite like kids, this is a bit annoying (and a bit dangerous). Of course, your newly mobile kid quite rightly feels cooped up in a highchair and is delightfully curious about the world around them, which is fine – let 'em stretch their legs and invite them on loo trips – but hold their hand as they go and ideally let them toddle outside, or at least away from the main dining area.

8. Know when to cut your losses

If your baby kicks off and nothing is helping, just take them outside. You will look like a responsible, caring, considerate mother and everyone will feel more relaxed. If this happens when you're still eating, get your food bagged up to finish at home. Remember, unlike unfinished Eggs Benedict, revenge is a dish best served cold: why not just write this off as a bad day and secretly vow to get outrageously drunk in front of all your child's friends at their eighteenth birthday party?

9. Feign a vague interest in clearing up

Look, we all know those baby wipes and that grubby muslin aren't going to cut it when it comes to clearing up the inevitable trail of destruction your little foodie will leave on, around and under the table, but don't just sneak off. Instead, half-heartedly pretend to clear up the mess – hey, maybe even politely ask for a cloth 'because I'm so mortified at how much mess my baby's made!' – and soon the staff will be swarming around you with industrial-sized brooms and mops that exist for this very purpose. You'll look like the bigger person and, more importantly, won't risk getting your food gobbed on, should you venture into the establishment again.

10. If all else fails ... heeeeeere's Peppa

Nobody likes how they feel when they resort to thrusting a screen into their kid's face to shut them up. Especially in public, because we want people to think we're amazing, hands-on, creative, engaged parents. But in some situations – plane journeys, hangovers – it's essential. Seriously, what did people do before the internet? *How did they have children?* It's unthinkable. So, anyway, if the toys have failed, the crayons have failed and the food has failed, whip out your device of choice and fire up YouTube/Netflix/the CBeebies app. Voilà, total silence ... well, apart from Daddy Pig's voice booming across the restaurant.

WHAT OUR MUM MATES SAY

I met a work friend – a childless man! – for lunch at a really busy cafe in central London when my little boy was a few months old, just big enough to go in a highchair. Unfortunately I didn't notice that said highchair – one of those low, dark brown wooden ones that lots of pubs and cafes have – didn't have the crucial strap between the legs. I was chatting away to my friend when I realised my baby had quietly slipped right down, and was basically dangling between the table and the highchair with just his head poking out of the gap for his feet. Not my finest parenting moment ...

Mary, mum of two

We took advantage of newborns not having a proper bedtime and took our baby out for dinner one evening. He was fast asleep in the sling – until the food arrived, of course, when he wanted a feed too. I was feeling quite smug, feeding my lovely baby and eating one-handed, but then suddenly he threw up. It covered his whole face, went in his eyes, up his nose, over his clothes and all over mine too. We did have a nice evening though!

Lucy, mum of three

Wispy hair and Popeye arms: weird stuff you'll notice about your body in the first year

As if being pregnant hadn't been freaky enough, it turns out there's a whole load of weird, unexpected physical side effects to being a mum in general that will make themselves known over the first few months. We all know about stretch marks and compromised boobs, but what else does having a baby do to your body?

Wispy hair

Remember that lustrous mane you rocked during pregnancy to distract everyone from your swollen fingers and shell-shocked face? *Gone.* Your hormones have been larking about again, resulting in hair loss a few months after giving birth – which may well be delayed if you're exclusively breastfeeding. Then starts the regrowth – the reasons why lots of new mums have strange wispy hairlines, and often drastic new haircuts. It all gets back to normal eventually. Well, unless you have another baby.

Messed-up teeth

In their ongoing bid to prematurely age you, babies also mess with your teeth while in utero, increasing your chances of gum disease and decay. You'll probably notice this a few months later ... hopefully not so many months later that your entitlement to free post-natal dental care has expired.

Massive feet

Feet can go up a size or two during pregnancy, in keeping with the rest of your body. But the kicker is, they sometimes stay that way, so you may find yourself blowing your mat pay on new shoes (flat, practical mum shoes, of course).

More manageable periods

If you had irregular, heavy or generally icky periods before having a baby, you might be in for a pleasant surprise when dear old Aunt Flo rears her ugly head in the months after giving birth (as an aside, if you're formula-feeding or combi-feeding, your periods could come back pretty promptly, whereas it tends to be around the nine-month mark for the average breastfeeding mum – although this varies massively because of pesky hormones). Generally, women report that their periods are lighter and less painful after having babies, and they can be more regular too. Hooray!

Bulging biceps

Here's another 'side effect' that should be celebrated – all that lugging around your baby has made you physically stronger than you've ever been (unless you were a professional body-builder pre-pregnancy, anyway). You'll notice that your arms are musclier than ever before without you even trying, and all that pacing around with a pram may well have given you thighs you could crack a nut with too. Whoop! *You are woman, hear you roar* (not now, though, the baby's sleeping).

WHAT OUR MUM MATES SAY

The teeth thing is so weird! I'd never had any issues and have always looked after my teeth well (we have dentists in the family so it was drummed into me from a young age) but after my first I started getting loads of aches and pains and ended up having to have a root canal.

Nicky, mum of two

I swear that my eyesight has deteriorated since I had my first baby. I had to get stronger glasses when he was a few months old after having the same ones for years. I can't find much scientific evidence of this, so it might just be down to sleep deprivation and ageing generally ... but then those are the baby's fault too ...

Mary, mum of two

Grapes, sockets and stairs: the hidden enemies of babies and how to handle them

'I won't let the house get taken over by baby stuff!' we all vow. Then the baby happens. And boy (or girl), does it happen. Soon, there are multi-coloured foam tiles where your stylish geometric rug used to be, and annoying plastic safety thingy-majigs making previously simple tasks take about twice as long.

But we live in what is essentially a colourful padded cell for a reason – we're desperate to keep our babies safe from danger. And when you become a mum, you realise that danger is everywhere, which means we can go a bit nutty with the babyproofing – to the point where our homes are kind of adult-proof too, since nobody wants to come round and have to drink out of sippy cups.

These are a few of the everyday items which will suddenly scream *'danger danger!'* and what you should do about them to try to keep your family alive and/or keep things in perspective.

Stairs

When your baby first gets mobile, your stairs will become a source of fascination to them. Stairgates are often the first babyproofing purchase new parents make – and generally the most expensive one. But they aren't always necessary; it all depends on the layout of your house – if there are strategically located doors, which mean that your baby can't get to the stairs unattended anyway, you might be better off making the most of this and focus on teaching them how to climb the stairs safely when you're around to supervise. Going downstairs is more dangerous anyway, so popping a gate at the top of the stairs can be far more valuable, especially when your 'baby' becomes an actual child, moves into a real bed and starts padding around in the dark at all hours, the little bugger!

Grapes

Ah, the simple grape. So small, so nutritious, so *deadly*. If you've ever been to a baby first-aid class, the instructors will have scared the bejesus out of you with all their chat about choking hazards, and grapes are at the top of the list. But you needn't banish them from your home for ever; you just need to always chop them lengthways (and maybe squish them a bit too). Crisis over.

The oven/other hot things

'Hot!' is a common first word for a reason – babies are constantly getting told to stay away from ovens/burning fires/ active volcanoes by us tedious, killjoy parents. It is difficult to baby-proof an oven (or indeed a volcano) since blocking it off renders it pretty useless when you want to, like, eat, but you can always shove a chair in front of it if your baby is knocking around in the kitchen while it's on. Otherwise you'll just have to embrace your new catchphrase: 'No! Hot! Don't touch! Hot!' ad nauseum.

The washing machine and other large appliances

Sure, we've all heard horror stories about small children getting trapped in washing machines, but in reality this is a pretty rare phenomenon. They're far more likely to simply fiddle with all the buttons and mess with your spin cycle, wreaking laundry schedule havoc on the entire household. Some washing machines have lock buttons to ward off meddling little fingers; if yours doesn't, again, it's just a case of teaching them not to. Or, more usefully, teaching them how to do it right, so you can sit back and relax while they wash their own stinking socks.

Plugs and sockets

A controversial one. Socket covers used to be another of
the first and most obvious babyproofing purchases parents
would make, but in recent years the NHS have urged families
not to buy them, because they actually make sockets *more*
dangerous – yes, really. The fact is, British sockets have been
designed so that even the smallest of fingers can't poke into
the holes, so we can all chill out on that front.

Cleaning products and other toxic liquids

While most nasty substances are sold in childproof contain-
ers, there's probably something evil lurking in your cupboard
that baby hands can get to. To be on the safe side, little plastic locks are cheaply and readily available, making it nigh
on impossible for your little one to pry their way into your
cupboard. The slight downside is that the more grown-up
members of the household may also find it nigh-on impossible to get into the cupboard. So the sink remains forever
filthy but, hey, at least we're all safe.

Coins and other pesky little things

No matter how much of a Marie Kondo job you do on your
house, you will never be able to rid it entirely of tiny little
choking hazards. Likewise, contactless payment might be
ubiquitous these days, but you've still got coins knocking
around, haven't you? At some point – perhaps even on a
daily basis, especially if they're teething – your baby will put

something in their mouth that's not supposed to be in their mouth. You will freak. But most stuff gets spat out (filthy pound coins don't actually taste that nice, who knew?) and if it doesn't ... well, you have a legitimate reason to go to A&E. Chances are, whatever they've ingested will pass safely through their system, and you'll change their nappy and come out with a cash prize, but some items are more dangerous than others: especially, annoyingly enough, those teeny little batteries which are often found in kids' toys, so always head to hospital if you're worried they've swallowed something dodgy.

WHAT OUR MUM MATES SAY

I went baby-proofing crazy when my first started crawling. We had bars and covers all around the house, it wasn't a pretty sight and I dread to think how much money we spent. He still got into scrapes, though, so I soon realised that you can't keep them safe from everything. We didn't really bother with our second, we just tried to teach her to be safe instead although most of her injuries were courtesy of her big brother anyway!

Becca, mum of two

In the first couple of years, we've been through broken bones, broken teeth and lots and lots of bumps and bruises. But almost all of these happened outside of our house! You can only protect them so much – adventurous kids will get into scrapes regardless.

Nicky, mum of two

You can't babyproof everything – one of my mum friends took her baby to A&E because they bashed their head on a chandelier while being swung around the room. Most middle-class injury ever?

Ruth, mum of one

Things mums can disagree on (but it doesn't mean you can't be friends)

Mum World is a lovely place, of course – full of cake and nursery rhymes and poo – but there are a few contentious issues that can cause disagreements between mum mates. Basically, we're all different kinds of parents – different kinds of humans, in fact – and as long as we're doing what makes us and our babies happy, it doesn't really matter a jot. However, when you're sleep-deprived and questioning every decision you make, you can lose sight of this and feel like you're being judged for the way you care for your baby.

Milk-dispensing methods

This old thing again. We all know that it technically doesn't matter how we choose to feed our own baby, but, because feeding them is so all-consuming, it is in our heads all the time, and we find ourselves utterly convinced that we're doing it the right way. Which, of course, we are ... for us. If you're still breastfeeding when most of your mum crowd have stopped, you can feel isolated – especially when they seem to have their 'lives back'. And if you're a formula-feeder, but all your crew are boobs-out, you can feel guilty and left out. Either way, there are groups out there where you can find like-minded mums – bosom buddies, or otherwise – including on Mush. Also, when feeding becomes less constant, it will soon all seem irrelevant anyway, so if you like your friends, hang in there!

Weaning

Some mums start their babies on solids a little sooner than the advised six months. Some mums spoon-feed. Some mums do baby-led weaning. Some mums buy pouches and microwave meals. Some take great pride in meticulously home cooking everything. Most mums just wing it. The majority of actual scientific research suggests your method of weaning has very little bearing on your kid's future eating habits, so it's really what you find works best for *you* and your family, and not Josie from Baby Yoga's family.

Sleeping quarters

Some mums swear by co-sleeping, which, as long as it's done within the safety guidelines, can be a way to get a lot more sleep in the early months. But some mums find that the whole household feels more rested if the baby moves to their own room sooner rather than later. Surely this is the ultimate in decisions that really only concern the people involved, right?

Crying it out

'I can't imagine ever leaving my baby to cry,' declare some mums, while others use controlled crying to bring a bit of routine into their lives. There are all sorts of studies into all this that are well worth reading up on if you're thinking of taking the plunge. But mum friends, however well-meaning, aren't always the best source of info on this one, since, in case you hadn't noticed by now, all babies are different, and all mums are differenter still.

Social media use

Some mums have dedicated Instagram accounts to show off their offspring's outfit *du jour*. Others implement a social media blackout and don't reveal anything about their baby, to the point where you didn't even know they had one. Most of us, though, are somewhere in between, popping up the odd, particularly cute photo, because do you know what? Our friends and family actually like it! Whichever camp you fall into, it doesn't matter – but if you get told off for posting a picture of your fiercely private pal's precious poppet, you can end up feeling a little bit told-off and judged. Don't – everyone's entitled to their own set of social media rules … just check next time!

Routine

This one can have practical implications on gangs of mates, with some new mums determined to have their babies napping on a schedule (and *definitely* at home in their cot) and going to bed at 7.00 pm from early on, while others wing it and let them doze in their buggies, should they be so inclined, even if this takes place at 9.00 pm in a pub. All of which is, again, fine, but it's worth seeking out extra mum mates who do things the same way as you, simply so you actually get company when you need it the most.

Screen time

Anyone had a mum round who's gently requested that the TV be switched off, because they don't like their little one seeing screens? It can make you feel awfully guilty if you're the kind who likes a bit of background CBeebies action at all times. Or, if you're the one implementing the screen-time ban, you can feel like you're being a bit precious. The truth is, both of you are entitled to do things your way, with no judgy pants required. Just maybe arrange the next playdate at an outdoor location.

Discipline

If you wince when your mate puts her kid on the naughty step or shouts at them in public, they're probably doing the same when you, in their eyes, let your little one get away with murder. Behaviour and discipline is a mega mum-minefield – and one that only increases as babies turn into toddlers and beyond – but the main rule is: don't tell off another mum's child unless you're prepared to deal with the consequences. The consequences often being said mum turning into an actual tiger.

WHAT OUR MUM MATES SAY

I wish I'd been a bit more chilled about my baby's routine, as I missed out on loads of stuff in the early months because I was rushing him home for naps while everyone else just let them doze in their buggies. I think they all thought I was nuts! Second time round I just went with the flow and had a much better daytime social life as a result.

Cathy, mum of two

I found it hard when all my mum friends were bottle-feeding or combi-feeding their babies after a few months. In general I was really happy and proud to still be breast-feeding but it meant they were ready for nights out before I was because I needed to feed my baby to sleep. In hindsight, it was a brief time of our lives and wasn't important, but at the time I felt a bit embarrassed – like they must think I was being clingy or something. It sounds so silly now – my baby was only three months old!

Izzy, mum of two

Five cheap and easy things to do when you've got cabin fever

Directionless days with little ones are difficult, but it's impossible to think of fun, creative stuff to do every day. When it's raining outside and the living room is a tip and the baby is wreaking havoc and you're just *desperate* to get out of the house but can't think of a thing to do, fear not – we're old pros at this stuff and have found a few ways to make those long days more bearable.

1. Charge around the pet shop

If you've got a big pet shop near you, you're laughing. You might think all those guinea pigs and goldfish are pretty boring, but your baby will be enchanted by them. Those £40 zoo tickets can wait until they're a bit older – when they're newly mobile, the pet shop is the perfect place for them to stumble around squealing at the animals. If you feel guilty for not spending money, it turns out some pet toys make pretty good baby toys too. We're not suggesting you shove a bone in your baby's mouth, but jangly balls are cheap and will offer hours of fun. Alternatively, you could buy some pet rats. Yeah, the ball doesn't seem like such a bad idea now, does it?

2. Join the library

So obvious, so often overlooked. And libraries aren't just full of books: most have free singing and craft classes for babies and toddlers too. Sign up when they're tiny and you'll have a go-to rainy day activity, plus you'll get warm, fuzzy vibes from feeling like you're supporting your local community.

3. Go camping

By which we mean, go camping in your own garden. Get yourself a cheap play tent (or use a real tent if you have one and can be bothered to erect it) and turn it into a den of dreams. A few cushions, a stack of books, some picnic foods and you and your little one can be at one with nature and escape the confines of the house without technically leaving it. A nice place for an afternoon nap too ... for both of you.

4. Ogle a building site

Not the most glamorous of locations, but little ones are oddly entranced by diggers and cement mixers and cranes and whatever all that other machinery's called, so find your nearest work in progress and go and stare at it – from a safe distance, of course. It just about counts as fresh air, if they're not doing anything involving noxious gases. You've probably been ogled by builders enough times – now it's payback.

5. Take a trip to the post box

Little kids love feeling like they're doing something important, so if you've got a birthday card to send or some admin to deal with, get them involved – let them scribble on the envelope and stick on the stamp and then set off to the post box. Kids love putting things in things, the weirdos, so this is the biggest part of the task at hand. Just make sure they don't post your phone and keys at the same time.

WHAT OUR MUM MATES SAY

I don't drive so on mat leave days when the weather was too rubbish to go to the park and none of my friends were around, I often struggled to find things to do – especially because I hate arts and crafts! But I gradually learned two things: 1. Babies don't care that it's pissing it down, plus they look really cute in wellies and puddle suits and 2. They are amused by the most mundane of things, so turning little tasks, like posting a letter, into an activity, is enough to keep them happy without spending any money!

Jo, mum of one

It's a weird one, but I've occasionally gone to car show-rooms when I've been at the end of my tether! I pretend we're looking for a new family car and then my little boy gets to run around, sit in the seats and play with all the buttons. The staff must hate us though ...

Becca, mum of two

Baby's first Christmas: how to use them to get you out of absolutely anything

Christmas is a time for celebration, relaxation and ... obligation. So. Much. Obligation. But a lot of that (especially the relaxation) is likely to change when you have a baby. Your first Christmas as a mum is a biggie – they won't remember a thing, but you very much will, so you might as well make the most of it. Here's how to use your new status to your advantage.

1. You can't go for drinkies and nibbles round Elaine and Clive at number 32's, the baby is sleeping. If Elaine and Clive at number 32 are so desperate to meet him/her, they can haul their middle-aged asses over here. And bring wine.

2. You feel terrible but you can't help with the cooking: the baby is going through a cluster feeding/clingy phase so you're basically stuck underneath them, weirdly until exactly twenty seconds before Christmas dinner is served when it's definitely Granny's job to hold them.

3. You're sorry for any inconvenience this may cause, but you can't all sit and watch the *Mrs Brown's Boys* Christmas special, you're strongly opposed to your little one watching TV at such a young age. Oh, but *Bake Off*'s OK, nice and calm. And they really like the *Strictly* music, so that's fine too. Just definitely no *Mrs Brown's Boys*.

4. You're gutted, but you can't go and queue outside Next at 4.00 am on Boxing Day. It's not a great time for you, but if Auntie Pat wants to pick up some cut-price sleepsuits while she's there, you guess you're OK with it.

5. You're sorry you forgot to buy your partner's obnoxious nephew a present – the baby kicked off every time you tried to go shopping and, er, something about the internet playing up.

6. No thanks, you won't have any of your father-in-law's special 'cheeky eggnog', you're breastfeeding, but ... oh, what's this I'm holding? No, no, it's definitely not Prosecco, it's just Shloer, *sooo* boring ... hic!

7. Oh no, you missed your Pictionary turn because you swear you heard the baby monitor going off ... and then you had to rock them back to sleep ... Yeah, it's weird that nobody else heard it, but mothers just have a sixth sense for these things.

8. You unfortunately must decline the kind Facebook event invitation to Christmas Eve cocktails with the bitches that bullied you at school, because something vague and self-deprecating about bedtime routines, but here's a photo clearly illustrating that your baby is cuter than theirs.

9. Sorry, you're probably being over-cautious, but you were worried the baby would grab and choke on the chocolate tree decorations so you had to move them. Into your stomach. As quickly as possible. Phew, crisis averted.

10. As much as it's super, super sexy when your sprout-scented, beer-breathed partner spoons you and growls 'Ho ho ho, it's time for Santa to empty his sack', it just wouldn't be right when the baby is sleeping in the same room and your parents are just down the hall. Maybe next year, babe.

WHAT OUR MUM MATES SAY

Being heavily pregnant at Christmas is even better than having a baby at Christmas. OK, so you can't get drunk, but you can eat as much as you like and demand that everyone comes to visit you rather than having to actually go anywhere (God forbid you venture more than fifteen minutes' drive from the hospital ...). And they won't expect you to do the cooking either – your bump is so big that you can't reach the oven anyway. Enjoy it, because next year will be VERY different!

Izzy, mum of two

Our baby was only a couple of months old when it was her first Christmas, so most of the toys she got were wasted on her. It was an excellent chance to chill out a bit while other people held her, though! And dress her up in humiliating costumes, of course ...

Luisa, mum of one

Why you shouldn't freak out about milestones

There have been mini-milestones all the way along, of course, from first smile to first roll to first solid poo (ah, sweet memories ...). But it's towards the end of the first year that the big ones start kicking in: the things that transform them from a largely useless baby (sorry. They're cute though! *So* cute!) to a still fairly useless but increasingly engaging and entertaining toddler. If your baby is doing things at a different pace to their pals, it can be hard not to feel anxious about it, and start frantically googling and comparing notes with every mum you meet. But chill! Babies do things when they damned well want to, thank you very much, and, at this stage, what they do when has very little bearing on the future.

You're freaking out about: Crawling

The situation Your friends are babyproofing the shit out of their houses, but your little one is still quite content to sit around grinning, happily playing with toys that are in arm's reach.

When to get advice Never. While the majority of babies crawl between six and twelve months, some skip this stage entirely, and bum-shuffle instead, or go straight to cruising. You can try to encourage them by enticing them with toys, but babies are stubborn little monkeys and will do what they want in their own time.

You're freaking out about: Walking

The situation You're convinced your baby's playmates will have run ten marathons before your baby deigns to make it across the other side of the room.

When to get advice When they're approaching two. So, way after you've passed this book onto a pregnant friend/taken it to the charity shop (how could you?). The average age that babies walk is around thirteen to fourteen months, but there is a *huge* amount of variation (and girls tend to walk slightly earlier than boys), with some strutting their stuff as young as eight or nine months and others staying put until way beyond eighteen months. If yours is at the more relaxed end of the scale, we strongly recommend trying to enjoy the relative calm of your days.

You're freaking out about: Talking

The situation They haven't made any discernible noises and you just want a conversation, FFS.

When to get advice Not for *ages*. Before eighteen months, most babies don't say much beyond 'mama', 'dada' and a few choice animal noises, if you're lucky. After this, their vocabulary explodes, and even more so when they get past two. It's at their two-year health check (which generally happens at more like two and a quarter) that you can raise any concerns and, if necessary, they will be referred to a speech and language specialist.

You're freaking out about: Stuff they can't do with their hands

The situation They seem a bit cack-handed, lacking dexterity with their toys or being a bit rubbish with a fork or spoon. You fear their future career as an internationally respected artist/musician/nail technician is hanging in the balance.

When to get advice Again, not until they're two, when this sort of thing will be checked up on by a health visitor. In the meantime, you can encourage them (and, if they're in child-care, get their carers in on it too) by playing with building blocks, shape sorters, bricks, puzzles, dough ... in fact, most of the toys aimed at this age group are all about the hands.

You're freaking out about: their size

The situation You can tell from the clothes size they're in, or by the comments you get from tactless strangers ('Ooh, she's a big lass' or 'Aww, isn't he tiny?') that your little or not-so-little one is above or below average size for their age, and that makes you worry.

When to get advice Whenever you like. Drop-in weighing clinics aren't just for newborns – you can take babies of any age, and request that they are weighed and measured, as well as raising any concerns with the health visitors. If your baby has drastically changed centiles since they were tiny, it doesn't mean there's anything wrong – common early feeding issues, the ups and downs of weaning and how active your baby is can all mean that things get skewed along the way.

WHAT OUR MUM MATES SAY

My little boy was quite a 'content' – OK, lazy – baby and didn't crawl until gone 11 months when some of his friends were already walking. While I appreciated that my life was way less exhausting as a result, I felt a bit frustrated at times and like he was missing out on tearing around playgrounds and what-not. He eventually walked at just after 15 months ... when my brother enticed him across the room with a slice of pizza. I barely even think about it now – I'm too busy chasing him everywhere now that he can run, jump and climb!

Liz, mum of two

I got a real bee in my bonnet about my baby not rolling over for ages. I was convinced there must be something wrong with him and kept googling it and finding the scariest answers. Turns out he just didn't like rolling, he mastered everything else just fine and ended up being one of the first of his friends to walk so I feel a bit silly about it now.

Lucy, mum of two

Beauty hacks for mums with no time

Remember when you used to idly spend your mornings curling your eyelashes and straightening your hair and that sort of nonsense? Well, now your morning routine is non-existent; your baby has taken full ownership of it. But it *is* actually possible to make yourself feel a bit readier to face the world, whether you're heading off to work or just getting a coffee with a mate. Or, of course, you can just renounce make-up and pretend it's a feminist statement rather than a time-saving exercise.

Never be knowingly without wipes

You've probably got them scattered around the house anyway, but don't just waste them on your baby's stinking bum; use them on your face too. When it comes to removing make-up, baby wipes can be more effective, not to mention gentler and nicer-smelling, than grown-up face wipes, and they're a good morning refresher too. Obviously in an ideal world we'd all cleanse, tone and moisturise but we're pretty sure the baby just swallowed an acorn, so STFU.

Wash some of your hair

You can save loads of time in the morning by tying back the rest of your hair and using the teensiest bit of shampoo to give your fringe a refresh. Haven't got a fringe? Well, now is the time to get one. Clean, shiny, bouncy bangs are a great distraction from the rest of you, and also cover up unruly eyebrows. Even if it was a bouncy bang that got you in this mess in the first place ...

Brush lip balm (or nipple cream!) on your eyebrows

If, however, your eyebrows *are* a priority, and you don't have time to get them professionally perfect, a quick once-over with some lip balm (applied with an old toothbrush, or just your finger) will keep them under control. Nipple cream does the job too, and we bet you've got some of that knocking around somewhere.

Use eyeshadow to cover grey hairs

If you're fair of hair, you probably haven't even noticed if you're going grey yet or not, but if you're a brunette, boy, will you know about it. And getting your hair coloured, whether you go posh at a salon or do a DIY job at home, is hard to squeeze in. You can drag out the time between them by using eyeshadow to cover up grey hairs. And, just to be clear, since we know how tired you are, we mean brown or black eyeshadow, not the electric-blue stuff lurking in your bedside table from your mate's eighties-themed thirtieth.

Raid the cutlery drawer

If you've got puffy eyes – and of course you've got puffy eyes, we've *all* got puffy eyes – holding a metal spoon under them can reduce the excess baggage. If the only clean spoon you can find is a pink plastic Peppa Pig one, however, this probably isn't going to work.

Always rock a red lip

A bold red lipstick suits pretty much everyone and is a most excellent distraction from everything else that's going on. Well, until your baby starts looking at you funny and then smears their filthy hand on it anyway.

Perfect the mum bun

If all else fails, always make sure you've got a hair bobble on your wrist so that a 'chic', 'timeless' (ha!) mum bun can be implemented in hair-mergencies.

WHAT OUR MUM MATES SAY

I always feel like a different person if my mouth is clean! If my lips have been neglected, I use a toothbrush to buff them up and make them redder.

Katie, mum of two

I've noticed that lots of mums seem to chop all their hair off when they have babies – partly because babies like pulling hair but partly because it's in theory lower-maintenance. In theory. I made this mistake and realised my silly hair was way harder work when it was short, poking out all over the place. I've grown it again now and I don't even have to dry it!

Becca, mum of one

The things you promise yourself you'll *never* do – but then end up doing anyway

We all have ideas about the kinds of parents we're going to be, learning from the perceived 'mistakes' we've seen friends and family make. Then the baby comes and *bam*! Turns out we were seriously deluded. To the mother who's never broken any of the vows on the list (*Really*? You should be the one writing a book), we salute you – to everyone else, we're right there with you and we don't care.

Obsess about everything

You think you'll be one of those laid-back, go with the flow types who takes their baby to the pub and doesn't let them take over their lives. The baby will just be a cute lifestyle accessory who will revel in adult company and you'll still be you, only wiser, more nurturing and perhaps just ever so slightly chubbier. You won't get hung up on baby stuff because that's boring and naff. Ha. We totally get this, because when you're pregnant (or even before), you just can't imagine the huge change – the Mumsition! – that you're about to go through. If you knew about it, you would freak the hell *out*. The fact is, even the coolest of cucumbers gets hung up on how often their baby feeds and sleeps and poos and then ends up talking about it all the fricking time with anyone who'll listen. It's normal. Embrace it.

Let them eat crap

We start out on our weaning journey with the best of intentions and most first-time mums are pretty strict for the first few months of it, making sure they feed their baby nothing but lots of nice wholesome fruit, veg and natural – perhaps even organic – foods. A cheeky fromage frais feels like the height of decadence. But then things get busy. When you visit a friend with an older kid and they offer up some orange squash when your baby has only ever had water and milk, you feel like you're being precious if you turn it down. And when your baby won't stop squawking in the post office queue and the only snack you have on hand is half a packet of crisps, you will reach for them. And you just wait until they work out what the ice-cream van's all about. But chill your boots. As long as every meal isn't a KFC mega-bucket, they'll probably be OK.

Shout at them

Your baby will behave nicely because you'll treat them with respect and maturity and have reasoned, grown-up conversations with them from day one, right? Newsflash: babies are self-motivated and irrational, and even the most calm and caring of earth mothers will occasionally lose their composure. When, for instance, you're both beyond exhausted yet your baby is refusing to nap, you'll do your best to stay chilled, but occasionally snapping and raising your voice is totally normal. You'll hate the way you sound (just like your mum, by any chance?) but it will happen. Just put it down to a bad day for both of you and try not to use the C word.

Bribe them

Similarly, when your baby starts veering towards toddler-hood, you'll find other ways to get them into line – ways that you used to think you'd never consider and may even have, whisper it, judged other parents for in the past. Bribing them with technology, snacks and toys are all go-to's for many parents. As long as you don't make a habit of it and instead simply pull the bribes out of the bag when you need them the most, your baby probably won't turn into a manipulative psychopath. Well, unless it runs in the family.

Fill your house with excessive plastic tat

We all have visions of our baby playing contentedly with stylish, overpriced wooden toys purchased from craft fairs and Scandinavian websites. Then we realise early on that the best way to amuse them is to shove them in an all-singing, all-dancing, all-flashing, all-beeping, all-battery-devouring plastic contraption that's bigger than our first car and makes them giggle their adorable little heads off. Don't panic, we won't tell your Instagram followers if you won't.

Conform to gender stereotypes

When you're pregnant, you'll moan about the amount of girls' clothes featuring pink, sparkly slogans about princesses and boys' clothes emblazoned with pictures of fire engines and tractors. Then the baby comes and we're just grateful for whatever we're given. Fast forward to the toy years, and the same thing happens again. If your little girl gravitates towards dolls, fairy dresses and bunny rabbits while your boy loves dinosaurs, football and mud, it's nothing you've done. Blame decades of social conditioning or maybe even good old mother nature.

Let them watch telly and play on your phone

We have nothing but respect for parents who manage to avoid screen time for as long as possible. But how on earth do they get anything done? Lots of kids' telly these days is actually educational (right?), we grew up watching it and turned out just fine (right?) and by the time they're old enough for school, they'll probably be required to have smartphones instead of fingers, so what's the harm in starting early? In an ideal world, we'd spend our days stimulating our kids with arts and crafts and books and ukuleles, but, in that ideal world, there's also a friendly robot who does all our laundry, cooks dinner and keeps an eye on our emails. Never. Gonna. Happen.

WHAT OUR MUM MATES SAY

I swore I'd never go on about my baby's naps and structure my life around them. I definitely wouldn't ever say 'she's so tired' or 'she's just teething' to excuse dreadfulness. Fast forward six months and not only did I do all of that but I'd also pace the streets non-stop for an hour and a half in the rain so she'd get 'two good sleep cycles'. FFS!

Nicky, mum of two

I think we put too much pressure on ourselves to be perfect parents these days. I grew up watching cartoons and eating Monster Munch, and I don't think it's had any major detrimental effects, and yet still I find myself trying to uphold really high standards for my kids. I did quite well sticking to my promises with my first but with my second there was no chance ... and so far they've both turned out OK!

Mary, mum of two

'Do you want another one?' How to handle the nosiest of questions

No sooner has your baby left the cosy confines of your body than people will start asking if you want another one. It's a funny old question – after all, if someone was looking bloated and exhausted after eating a large pizza, you wouldn't offer them up the menu straight away for seconds, would you? As your baby gets older, and particularly as you approach their first birthday, the frequency of this line of questioning will increase, until you feel like you're being probed about it every bleeding day. Here's how to handle it whatever the circumstances.

You're secretly pregnant again already

What to say Well, it depends how well you know the person. If you've managed to get pregnant again when your baby is still a baby – maybe even when they're only a few months old (hello, Irish twins!) – people will assume it's an accident, even if this isn't the case at all. Either way, it's not really any of their business. Announce the news whenever you're ready, ignore the horrified looks and perfect your spiel about how you want to get the difficult bit out of the way in one go. Perfect.

You'd love another one, but you're not sure it's going to happen

What to say Remember that the asker of the question isn't trying to be insensitive – they've probably got no idea that conceiving number one was a battle, or that you've had miscarriages, or simply that you're worried you might be too old to have another one. Again, it depends who's asking – being brutally honest won't go down well with everyone, but it might make them think twice before they ask the question of anyone else.

You do want another one, just not right now

What to say No drama here – this is the most common state of affairs for most mums of under-ones, so you can just be honest, or mutter something about not being sure yet. The most common age gap between siblings is around the three-year mark, which means most parents aren't ready again until their first baby is turning two or thereabouts. And it's not a coincidence that three is also when subsidised childcare kicks in for most families.

You and your partner can't agree on it

What to say If one of you wants another baby but the other isn't so sure, things can get seriously tense. If, for instance, you're the one who's broody, you might take your partner's reluctance as a personal insult: do they not think you're up to it, and have they secretly found this whole parenting thing totally miserable? If it's the other way round, you might feel pressured to be a breeder when you're enjoying getting parts of your old life back. And none of this is anyone else's business, so going for the 'not sure yet' line is probably the best policy here as well ... until one of you gives in, anyway.

You don't want another one, actually

What to say Only children used to be a relatively rare phenomenon, but have increased in recent years due to couples starting families later – not to mention financial pressures. But still, some people don't quite get it, and will openly say really rude things about finding it 'cruel' to deprive little ones of siblings, which is obviously utterly ridiculous. Depending on how confident you feel in your decision, you could take this as a chance to educate them. Or you could just fall back on the whole 'not sure yet' thing too.

WHAT OUR MUM MATES SAY

We're definitely stopping at one. I didn't enjoy the new baby days and I know I don't want to do it again, and luckily my husband agrees. Our toddler has loads of friends and cousins around the same age, so the idea that we're depriving him is ridiculous, and I'm quite happy to tell people that! I'm actually enjoying being a mum a lot more since we've made this decision, too.

Laura, mum of one

I was three months pregnant with our second at our first baby's first birthday party, so we took the opportunity to announce it to our families and close friends. They were pretty surprised, but I'd gone back to work at six months, so everything felt accelerated. The early days of having two under two were obviously pretty hard but now that they're a bit older it's lovely having an eighteenth-month age gap.

Sarah, mum of two

Boom! You made it! Why their first birthday is really all about you

Whoosh, what a year. You did it! You're knackered, but you did it! Now, if your baby's first birthday is looming, chances are you're planning some kind of celebration. Whether it's a quiet, family-only affair at home or an enormous mash-up in your local soft-play hell, the important thing to bear in mind is: *Your baby, no matter how advanced they are, hasn't got the foggiest idea what's going on.*

Sure, buy them the ride-on toy of their dreams, bake them a cake featuring their favourite TV character – not that they ever watch TV, of course, ahem – but remember to take some time to celebrate surviving your first year as a mum too.

Whether you've loved every minute of it (really? *Every* minute?) or found the Mumsition tougher than you imagined, realising that you and your baby have muddled along together for a *whole year* can make you feel surprisingly emotional.

Just make sure you get some nice photos taken before you ruin your make-up, yeah?

And congratulations!

INDEX